SACRED TEXTS AND AUTHORITY

THE PILGRIM LIBRARY
OF WORLD RELIGIONS

SACRED TEXTS AND AUTHORITY

EDITED BY JACOB NEUSNER

The Pilgrim Press
Cleveland, Ohio

The Pilgrim Press, Cleveland, Ohio 44115
© 1998 by Jacob Neusner

Excerpts from *The Laws of Manu,* trans. Wendy Doniger with Brian K. Smith, 1991, used by permission of Penguin UK. Excerpts from *Sources of Indian Tradition,* 2d. ed., vol. 1, ed. Ainslee T. Embree, copyright © 1988, Columbia University Press, used by permission of Columbia University Press. We have made every effort to trace copyrights on the materials included in this publication. If any copyrighted material has nevertheless been included without permission and due acknowledgment, proper credit will be inserted in future printings after receipt of notice.

03 02 01 00 99 98   5 4 3 2 1

Library of Congress Cataloging-in-Publication Data
Sacred texts and authority / edited by Jacob Neusner.
     p.   cm. — (The Pilgrim library of world religions)
    Includes bibliographical references.
    ISBN 0-8298-1249-0 (pbk. : alk. paper)
    1. Sacred books. I. Neusner, Jacob, 1932– . II. Series.
BL71.S22 1998
291.8'2—dc21   97-46834
                                          CIP

CONTENTS

The great world religions address certain existential issues in common, for the human situation raises compelling questions that transcend the limits of time, space, and circumstance. Recognizing that each religion forms a system with its own definitive traits, we aver that all religions must and do treat in common a range of fundamental topics as well, and we hold that comparison and contrast among religions begins in the treatment of urgent questions that all of them must resolve. This library introduces the religions of the world as they meet in conversation on the profound issues of world order—transcendent, individual and familial, and social. In the first rubric falls how we know God; in the second, our life of suffering and death, women, and the aspiration for afterlife; and in the third, the authority and continuity of tradition itself. Indeed, for the purpose of these volumes we may define religion as a theory of the social order that addresses from the unique perspective of transcendence (God, in concrete language) issues of the human condition of home and family on the one side, and issues of the public interest on the other.

The five topics of the initial account require only brief clarification. Common to the human condition is the quest for God. Every religion identifies authoritative teaching ("sacred texts"), though what the various religions mean by "a text" will vary, since a person or a drama or a dance as much as a piece of writing may form a fixed and official statement for amplification and exegesis through time. One-half of humanity is comprised of women. Everyone suffers and everyone dies. Humanity everywhere aspires to explain what happens after we die. In these five volumes, the initial set in the Pilgrim Library of World Religions, we take up the five topics we deem both critical and ubiquitous in the religions we identify as paramount. Following a single outline, worked out in common, we spell out how each religion addresses the topic at hand. In this way we propose to make possible a labor of comparison of religions: how all address a single issue, uniformly defined.

The religions are chosen because all of them not only speak to humanity in common but also relate to one another in concrete, historical ways. Judaism, Christianity, and Islam join together in a common doctrine, the unity of God, and in valuing a common scripture, the Hebrew Scriptures of ancient Israel that Judaism knows as the written Torah—which is the Old Testament of Christianity, joined in the case of Christianity and Islam into the Bible, the book, comprising the Old and New Testaments. Hinduism forms the matrix out of which Buddhism took shape, much as ancient Israelite Scriptures amplified by the Judaism of the day defined the matrix in which Christianity originated. Not only do Judaism, Christianity, and Islam conduct an ongoing dialogue between and among themselves, but Christianity and Islam compete in Africa, and Hinduism and Islam in India. All five religions not only address humanity but reach across the boundaries of ethnic groups and local societies and speak of the condition of humanity. And all five come to formulation in a set of writings deemed classical and authoritative.

That fact—that each of the religions treated here identifies a canon that defines the faith—makes the work possible. For each of the religions treated here proves diverse; viewed over time, all of them yield marks of historical change and diversity of doctrine and practice alike. Take Judaism, for example. Today it breaks down to a number of distinct religious systems or Judaisms—Reform, Orthodox, and Conservative in North America, for instance. Christianity yields three vast divisions,

Catholic, Protestant, and Orthodox. The world has gotten to know some of the differences between Shiite and Sunni Islam. The upshot is that while we recognize the density and diversity of each of the religions under study in these volumes, our account of their principal doctrines on critical and universal issues appeals only to those writings that all forms or versions of the several religions acknowledge, to which all Judaisms or Christianities, for instance, will appeal.

That same fact—the appeal to authoritative writings of a classical character—also permits us to describe without nuance of context or historical circumstance the positions of the five religions. People who practice the religions set forth here may believe diverse things within the framework of those religions, respectively; Catholics may practice birth control, for example. So too, religions that bear a distinctive relationship to a given ethnic group—Judaism to Jews, for instance—cannot be defined merely by public-opinion polling of that ethnic group. Not all Jews practice Judaism, and not all Arabs Islam, nor all Italians Catholicism. By concentrating on the classical statements of the religions at hand, we set forth an ideal type, the picture of the religion that its authoritative writings provide, not the picture of the religion that the workaday world may yield.

The same consideration affects the diversity over time and in contemporary life of the several religions before us. Everyone understands that all five religions not only produced diverse systems, but also developed and changed over time, so that a doctrine or belief on a given topic in one time and place may not conform to the shape of the same doctrine or belief on the same topic in a different setting. For example, ideas about God vary, depending on the situation of the interpreter—learned or mystic or simple, for instance—or on the age in which the idea is explained. That is quite natural, given the vast stretches of time and space traversed by the five religions we examine.

While acknowledging the variations produced by the passage of time and the movement of culture, we appeal to the classical writings for an account that all later generations of the faithful, wherever located, can affirm, however diverse the interpretations placed upon that account. In the section immediately following this preface, Literary Sources of the World Religions, each of the writers lists the documents that form the foundation of his or her chapter in this volume.

This library took shape in the shared intellectual adventure that joins us together as professors of the academic study of religion at Bard College and in dialogue with our students there, and we tried out the various chapters on those students. The chapters were outlined in common. The writers of the substantive chapters further invited William Scott Green of the University of Rochester to read and introduce their discussions and to write conclusions, spelling out the results of putting side by side systematic accounts of how the five religions respond to exactly the same set of questions. Our respect for his intellectual leadership in the academic study of religion is amply vindicated in the result.

All of us express our appreciation to the president of Bard College, Dr. Leon Botstein, and dean of faculty Stuart Levine, for their encouragement of this project; and to Mr. Richard Brown, then of Pilgrim Press, our patient and gentle editor, whose good ideas always made the work still more challenging and stimulating than our joint venture had made it to begin with. Mr. Timothy Staveteig, our new editor at Pilgrim Press, has continued the tradition of the helpful and gentle editor, deftly shaping our work. Finally, the editor expresses special thanks to both the University of South Florida for the privilege of a distinguished research professorship and to Bard College for the pleasure of a professorship shaped to my circumstances.

Jacob Neusner
SERIES EDITOR

CONTRIBUTORS

JONATHAN BROCKOPP received his Ph.D. from Yale University and is assistant professor of religion and chairman of the department of religion at Bard College.

BRUCE CHILTON is Bernard Iddings Bell Professor of Religion and chaplain of Bard College and is rector of the Free Church of St. John the Evangelist.

BRADLEY S. CLOUGH is a Ph.D. candidate at Columbia University and is visiting assistant professor of Asian studies and religion at Bard College.

WILLIAM SCOTT GREEN founded the department of religion and classics at the University of Rochester and is now dean of the college.

JACOB NEUSNER is distinguished research professor of religious studies at the University of South Florida and professor of religion at Bard College.

BRIAN K. SMITH is professor of religious studies at the University of California, Riverside.

The Pilgrim Press is a leading publisher in Christian ethics and theology. Through the Pilgrim Library of World Religions series, edited by Jacob Neusner, we seek to continue and expand this heritage.

Part of this heritage is a policy regarding the use of inclusive language for human beings and for God. With few exceptions, the Pilgrim Library of World Religions maintains this heritage. Nevertheless we recognize that various religious traditions have struggled differently with inclusive language for God. Therefore each contributor, especially when discussing God's self-revelation, has been offered some flexibility in order to faithfully reflect that religious tradition's current form of expression.

INTRODUCTION

One of the most commonplace images in American life surely is the picture of the President of the United States taking the oath of office with his hand on a Bible. It used to be typical—and in many locations apparently still is—for people called to testify in an American courtroom to place a hand on a Bible and swear "to tell the whole truth and nothing but the truth, so help me God." These actions seem so familiar to us that we often miss their implications. In these very ordinary rites of secular American life, a person swears an oath or makes a vow to do something—in the cases above, to uphold the Constitution or to tell the truth. The gesture of placing a hand on the Bible signifies that the person in question intends to keep the promise he or she has made. The Bible is the guarantor of the promise.

The Bible is the guarantor of the promise? How can that be? Can a book, printed on ordinary paper on a standard printing press, guarantee anything? For any other book, that would be a good question. But in the West—particularly in America—the Bible has a special status. In the form of the Hebrew Scriptures and the New Testament, the Bible is the scripture of Christianity, the dominant religion of Western culture. In the form of the Hebrew Scriptures alone, the Bible is the scripture of Judaism, the religion out of which Christianity emerged. As such, the Bible is assumed by many—in America, perhaps even by the majority—to contain the teachings of God. Indeed, in many forms of Christianity, the Bible is called the Word of God. The swearing of oaths on, or in front of, a religion's scripture is neither new nor uniquely Christian. In ancient times both Jews and Christians made vows in front of the Torah scroll, which is part of Judaism's scripture. At the very least, to place one's hand on the Bible and swear an oath is to invoke God as a witness to the oath. The act suggests that a failure to fulfill the vow is an act of bad faith to God, and that serious consequences can, indeed will, follow. Because of its status as the scripture of a religion—the repository of the religion's fundamental teachings—the Bible is assumed to represent, and perhaps to contain—a superhuman power that should not be transgressed. Societies that hold this and comparable beliefs assume that people will swear an oath on the Bible only if they mean it and intend to keep it. In this sense, the Bible can be the guarantor of a promise—a very effective one, indeed. It is powerful because it is a sacred text. Even in our largely secular world, the idea of a sacred text still has resonance and relevance. This example of the use of a sacred text in our own world can help to open a door to the issues raised in this anthology.

As the chapters in this book demonstrate, the great literate religions of the world—Judaism, Islam, Buddhism, Hinduism, Christianity—all have writings that they judge to be authoritative for living the religious life. Typically, something about the way these texts are produced, treated, and maintained distinguishes them from all other writing. The sacred text may be written in a unique way; it may be memorized; it may be recited or chanted on ritual and liturgical occasions; it may be interpreted with methods applied to no other writings. Sacred texts usually claim, or are deemed by their devotees, to go beyond history, to have a superhuman source, to contain true teachings. In other words, sacred texts are endlessly applicable. In principle, they cannot be made historically relative or made irrelevant. In all ages, they are able to speak to the present. The capacity to be eternally pertinent marks sacred texts off from other writings.

Sacred texts may be endlessly applicable, but it does not follow that they are universally accessible, even within their own religious community. Although the religions discussed in this volume are literate, for most of history the bulk of their adherents were not. This means that the majority of the practitioners of Judaism, Islam, Buddhism, Hinduism, and Christianity did not read the Torah scroll, the Qur'ān, the Lotus Sutra (to cite but one possible Buddhist text), the *Rig Veda* (*Ṛg Veda*), or the New Testament. Even now, when literacy is widespread but not ubiquitous, it is not clear that most practitioners of the religions discussed in this book "read" the sacred texts of their religion in any systematic or disciplined way. More typically, religious intellectuals and virtuosi read, understand, interpret, mediate, and exemplify the texts in the life of a religious community. Hence, a persisting theme in the chapters below is the way the authority of a sacred text—which itself frequently (but not always) derives from the superhuman source of the text—is transferred to a religious expert who becomes, often in the language of the religion itself, a "living" text. These "living" texts become models of behavior—of ethics, piety, learning, compassion, and discipline. People who practice those religions turn to these "living texts" to learn what to do and what their religion teaches.

But texts—written and "living"—are not the only components of religious authority that surround the phenomenon of sacred writings. There are also the matters of interpretation and tradition. Perhaps the best way to demonstrate these is to repeat—with apologies—a rendering published at least twenty years ago by the great American cartoonist Jules Feiffer. In his cartoon, Feiffer depicted a young, long-haired woman in a leotard, sitting on the ground with knees bent, her head resting in her arms on her knees. A group standing behind her asserts, "You are our leader!" She replies, "I am not your leader." The group becomes more insistent. "You are our leader!" they call out. "I am *not* your leader!" she rejoins. "*You are our leader!*" they cry. "I am *not* your leader," she screams, "I am *nobody's* leader." The group is stunned, silent. Then one member of the group turns to the others and says, "No bodies! She said we have no bodies!" "That means we are ethereal beings," says one. "That means we are angels," says another. And the group turns inward, busily discussing the implications of what they have just heard. The woman gradually notices that the group has lost interest in her. She approaches them and shouts, "*I am not your leader.*" One member of the group turns outward from the circle the group has formed. "Bug off, leader," he says firmly, "we're interpreting."

All the religions considered below have developed methods, criteria, and communities of the interpretation of sacred texts. The criteria used to judge an interpretation authentic vary not only from religion to religion, but also from group to group within a given religion. Religions that claim historical founders often develop a chain of tradition that goes back to the founder or one of his disciples. In those cases, historical proximity to the founder is the criterion of authenticity. Other groups or teachers will appeal to human reason, or to the clarity of teaching, or to consistency among sacred texts, or to the efficacy of a given text. Likewise, religions that claim historical founders sometimes will develop a set of teachings attributed to the founder but not included in the sacred texts themselves. In such instances, the religions typically develop means to associate—to the point of identity—the nontextual teachings with the sacred texts themselves. Different modes and methods of interpretation tend to be promulgated over time in schools or communities, so that none of the religions considered in this book can claim a uniform understanding of its sacred texts among its adherents. Within each religion there are conflicting schools of interpretation, which apply and appropriate sacred texts in different, sometimes irreconcilable ways. Feiffer's pithy "Bug off! We're interpreting!" is amply demonstrated in the pages to come. Interpretive traditions can easily take on a life of their own.

As with other volumes in this series, one of the reader's obligations is to use the discrete chapters to assess the analytical value of the broad category that brings them together. The evidence of the varied religions shows that they do not treat what we call "sacred texts" in the same way, and it is important for us to remember that even a category as neutral-sounding as "sacred text" carries intellectual and ideological baggage. All these religions have authoritative texts, but the texts are not necessarily authoritative for the same reasons or in the same ways, and it would be a mistake to begin reading with that assumption. Finally, it may be helpful to point out that although the religions discussed in this series appear in a different order in each volume—and although the religions grew and developed alongside one another—there is a historical relationship among them. Christianity emerged with cognizance of Judaism and its scripture, but not the reverse. Islam developed with full awareness of both Judaism and Christianity and their scriptures, but not the reverse. Likewise, Buddhism emerged from Hinduism, and not the reverse. Some readers and teachers may prefer to read these chapters using that sequence.

To conclude, let us return to our initial example. What makes the sacred texts of religions powerful is the distinctive range and scope of the appeal religion makes to human beings. The attraction and persistence of religions lie partially, if not principally, in their conviction of the fundamental correctness of their vision of reality, which both shapes and is generated by their adherents' experience in the world. Religions are compelling because of their affirmations of certitude and truth, because of their refusal to compromise on basic convictions, and because of the extent of their claims on the human person. Unlike other aspects of culture—politics or philosophy, for example—religion tends to extend its reach, to be comprehensive in scope. In nearly all societies, the cultural construction we call religion exhibits enormous range of expression. For instance, religion attacks all the senses—not only in speech and writing, but also in art, music, and dance, in smell and taste, in ethics, sexuality, and intellect. Most religions have cosmologies and eschatologies, theories of nature, birth, gender, marriage, suffering, and death. Which political system, social ideology, or philosophy has such a reach or exhibits religion's capacity to make definitive demands on the total human being? Sacred texts—and the authority that flows from and surrounds and complements them—epitomize the distinctive demands and visions of religions, and therefore they can help us keep a promise.

CHAPTER I

Judaism

HOW DOES JUDAISM MAKE ITS ENDURING STATEMENTS? WHAT EXACTLY DOES JUDAISM MEAN BY A TEXT?

Judaism knows God through God's self-manifestation in the Torah, and Judaism meets God in the Torah. We recall that the record of the meeting—the Torah itself—takes shape both in writing and in oral tradition, through memory. Accordingly, a certain set of books, those in the Hebrew Scriptures, form only part of the record; another part is comprised of unwritten traditions, oral traditions, that learned sages may themselves not only transmit but formulate on their own, in response to the learning and logic of their own mastery of the Torah.

It follows that Judaism makes its enduring statements in response to, in relationship with, the Torah, and by "a text," this religion means only "Torah." But "Torah" stands for divinely revealed truth, and the particular realization, in the here and now, of that truth, may take more than written form. The conception that the Torah of Sinai is formulated orally and transmitted in memory, not only written in scrolls, opens the way to the conception that people will understand "text" to mean any permanent form of preserving the record of Sinai, and, moreover, any lesson that belongs within that revelation. How a given sage acts, as much as what he says, forms part of the

Torah. What an authoritative sage says on his own authority may find its place within the tradition of Sinai. It follows that just as Judaism receives the Torah in an open-ended chain of tradition, each generation joining the labor in its turn, so Judaism regards its canon—the collection of authoritative writings—as never closed but always open.

A particular way of expressing the conception of sacred truth as a matter of status—what belongs to authoritative tradition—rather than of canonical acceptance in a limited collection of books is indicated by the use of the word *Torah*. By "the Torah" people may well mean, "the Five Books of Moses," or "the Hebrew Scriptures" (aka "the Old Testament"). Some may even include within "the Torah" the documents that preserve in writing the originally oral revelation of Sinai, some of which we shall meet later in this chapter. But when the word loses its definite article and becomes "Torah," it refers to a matter of status, assigning to the standing of Torah the lessons of the newest generation of sages, the teachings of the fresh morning.

Judaism as we know it at the end of late antiquity reached its now familiar definition when "the Torah" lost its capital letter and definite article and ultimately became "torah." A simple story conveys this usage and shows us what is at stake:

> It has been taught on Tannaite authority:
> Said R. Aqiba, "I once went after R. Joshua to the privy and I learned the three things from him.
> "I learned that people defecate not on an east-west axis but on a north-south axis.
> "I learned that one urinates not standing but sitting.
> "And I learned that one wipes not with the right hand but with the left."
> Said Ben Azzai to him, "Do you behave that insolently toward your master?"
> He said to him, "It is a matter of Torah, which I need to learn."

It has been taught on Tannaite authority:

Ben Azzai says, "I once followed R. Aqiba into the privy, and I learned three things from him:

"I learned that people defecate not on an east-west axis but on a north-south axis.

"And I learned that people urinate not standing up but sitting down.

"And I learned that people wipe themselves not with the right hand but with the left."

Said R. Judah to him, "Do you behave all that insolently toward your master?"

He said to him, "It is a matter of Torah, which I need to learn."

R. Kahana went and hid under Rab's bed. He heard [Rab and his wife] "conversing" and laughing and doing what comes naturally. [Cunnilingus being performed,] he said to him, "It appears that Abba's mouth has never before tasted 'the dish.'"

He said, "Kahana, are you here! Get out! That's disgraceful!"

He said to him, "It is a matter of Torah, which I need to learn."

—Bavli Berakhot 62A

The conduct of the master at home, in the privy and the bedroom, not only the teachings in the classroom, represented Torah-teaching, and the master embodied the Torah. Now the Torah, which for long had been a particular scroll or book, thus came to serve as a symbol of an entire system. Indeed, the word not only loses its definite article but its capital letter. When a rabbi spoke of torah, he no longer meant only a particular object, a scroll and its contents. Now he used the word to encompass a distinctive and well-defined worldview and way of life. Torah had come to stand for something one does. Knowledge of the Torah promised not merely information about what people were supposed to do, but ultimate redemption or salvation.

If, therefore, the particular text of Judaism, the Torah, contains the enduring statement of faith, exactly what people meant by "the Torah" serves as a talisman to record the history of Judaism. The Torah of Moses clearly occupied a critical place in all systems of Judaism from the closure of the Torah-book, the Pentateuch, in the time of Ezra onward. But in late antiquity, for one group alone the book developed into an abstract and encompassing symbol, so that in the Judaism that took shape in the formative age, the first seven centuries of the common era, everything was contained in that one thing.

When we speak of Torah, in rabbinical literature of late antiquity, in line with the stories we have just noted, we no longer denote a particular book, on the one side, or the contents of such a book on the other. Instead, we connote a broad range of clearly distinct categories of noun and verb, concrete fact and abstract relationship alike. "Torah" stands for a kind of human being. It connotes a social status and a sort of social group. It refers to a type of social relationship. It further denotes a legal status and differentiates among legal norms. As symbolic abstraction, the word encompasses things and persons, actions and status, points of social differentiation and legal and normative standing, as well as "revealed truth." In all, the main points of insistence of the whole of Israel's life and history come to full symbolic expression in that single word. If people wanted to explain how they would be saved, they would use the word *Torah*. If they wished to sort out their parlous relationships with gentiles, they would use the word *Torah*. Torah stood for salvation and accounted for Israel's this-worldly condition and the hope, for both individual and nation alike, of life in the world to come. For the kind of Judaism under discussion, therefore, the word *Torah* stood for everything. The Torah symbolized the whole, at once and entire. When, therefore, we wish to describe the unfolding of the definitive doctrine of Judaism in its formative period, the first exercise consists in paying close attention to the meanings imputed to a single word.

Every detail of the religious system at hand exhibits essentially the same point of insistence, captured in the simple notion of the Torah as the generative symbol, the total, exhaustive expression of the system as a whole. That is why the definitive ritual of the Judaism under study consisted in studying the Torah. The definitive myth explained that one who studied Torah would become holy, like Moses "our rabbi," and like God, in whose image humanity was made and whose Torah provided the plan and the model for what God wanted of a humanity created in God's image. As for Christians it was in Christ that God was made flesh, so the framers of the system of Judaism at hand found in the Torah that image of God to which Israel should aspire, and to which the sage in fact conformed.

The meaning of the several meanings of the Torah should require only brief explanation.

1. When "the Torah" refers to a particular thing, it is to a scroll containing divinely revealed words.
2. The Torah may further refer to revelation, not as an object but as a corpus of doctrine.
3. When one "does Torah" the disciple "studies" or "learns," and the master "teaches," Torah. Hence while the word *Torah* never appears as a verb, it does refer to an act.
4. The word also bears a quite separate sense, torah as category or classification or corpus of rules, e.g., "the torah of driving a car" is a usage entirely acceptable to some documents. This generic usage of the word does occur. It then means, "the teaching."
5. The word *Torah* very commonly refers to a status, distinct from and above another status, as "teachings of Torah" as against "teachings of scribes." For the two Talmuds that distinction is absolutely critical to the entire hermeneutic enterprise. But it is important even in the Mishnah.

6. Obviously, no account of the meaning of the word *Torah* can ignore the distinction between the two Torahs, written and oral. It is important only in the secondary stages of the formation of the literature.

7. Finally, the word *Torah* refers to a source of salvation, often fully worked out in stories about how the individual and the nation will be saved through Torah. In general, the sense of the word "salvation" is not complicated. It is simply salvation in the way in which Deuteronomy and the Deuteronomic historians understand it: Kings who do what God wants win battles, those who do not, lose. So too here, people who study and do Torah are saved from sickness and death, and the way Israel can save itself from its condition of degradation also is through Torah.

The symbolization of the Torah proceeds from its removal from the framework of material objects, even from the limitations of its own contents, to its transformation into something quite different and abstract, quite distinct from the document and its teachings. The Torah stands for this something more, specifically, when it comes to be identified with a living person, the sage, is endowed with those particular traits that the sage claimed for himself.

The Torah as the Holy Scriptures of Ancient Israel

The broadening of the meanings imputed to the word *Torah,* and the consequent redefinition of the canon of Judaism began with the first piece of writing after Scripture that was accepted as authoritative and holy. It is the Mishnah, a philosophical law code that reached closure c. 200 C.E. When the authors of the Mishnah surveyed the landscape of Israelite writings down to their own time, they saw only Sinai, that is, what we now know as Scripture. Beyond Scripture they acknowledged no writing prior to their own. They accepted as divine revelation also the Prophets and the Writings, to which they occasionally make reference. That they regarded the Torah, Prophets, and Writings as a single composition—that is, as revelation—appears from their references to the Torah as a specific "book" and to a Torah-scroll. Accordingly, one important meaning associated with the word *Torah* was concrete in the extreme. The Torah was a particular book or sets of books, regarded as holy, revealed to Moses at Sinai. That fact presents no surprise, since the Torah-scroll(s) had existed, it is generally assumed, for many centuries before the closure of the Mishnah in 200. So the concrete and physical meaning attaching to the word *Torah*—that is, the Torah, the Torah revealed by God to Moses at Mount Sinai (including the books of the Prophets and the Writings)—bore a contrary implication. Beyond the Torah there was no torah. Besides the Pentateuch, Prophets, and Writings, not only did no physical scroll deserve veneration, but no corpus of writings demanded obedience. So the very limited sense in which the words "the Torah" were used passed a stern judgment upon everything else, all the other writings that we know circulated widely, in which other Jews alleged that God had spoken and said "these things."

The Torah as an Activity—Where and How We Meet God

Tractate Abot, which reached closure about a generation after the Mishnah and was attached to it, in the aggregate differs from the Mishnah. The other sixty-two tractates of the Mishnah contain Torah-sayings here and there. But they do not fall within the framework of Torah-discourse. They speak about other matters entirely. The consideration of the status of Torah rarely pertains to that speech. Abot, by contrast, says a great deal about Torah-study. The claim that Torah-study produces direct encounter with God forms part of the tractate's thesis about the Torah.

R. Hananiah b. Teradion says, "[If] two sit together and between them do not pass teachings of Torah, lo, this is a seat of the scornful, as it is said, 'Nor sits in the seat of the scornful' (Psalms 1:1). But two who are sitting, and words of Torah do pass between them, the Presence is with them, as it is said, 'Then they that feared the Lord spoke with one another, and the Lord hearkened and heard, and a book of remembrance was written before him, for them that feared the Lord and gave thought to His name' (Malachi 3:16). I know that this applies to two. How do I know that even if a single person sits and works on Torah, the Holy One, blessed be he, sets aside a reward for him? As it is said, 'Let him sit alone and keep silent, because he has laid it upon him' (Lamentations 3:28)."

—Tractate Abot 3:2–3

In tractate Abot, Torah is instrumental. The figure of the sage, his ideals and conduct, forms the goal, focus, and center. To state matters simply: tractate Abot regards study of Torah as what a sage does. The substance of Torah is what a sage says. That is so whether or not the saying relates to scriptural revelation. The content of the sayings attributed to sages endows those sayings with self-validating status. The sages usually do not quote verses of Scripture and explain them, nor do they speak in God's name. Yet, it is clear, sages talk Torah. What follows? It is this: if a sage says something, what he says is Torah. More accurately, what he says falls into the classification of Torah. Accordingly, as I said, Abot treats Torah-learning as symptomatic, an indicator of the status of the sage, hence, as I said, as merely instrumental.

To spell out what this means, let us look at the opening sentences of tractate Abot:

Moses received Torah at Sinai and handed it on to Joshua, Joshua to elders, and elders to prophets. And prophets handed it on to the men of the great assembly. They said three things: "Be prudent in judgment. Raise up many disciples. Make a fence for the Torah."

—Tractate Abot 1:1

"Moses received Torah," and it reached "the men of the great assembly." The "three things" those men said bear no resemblance to anything we find in written Scripture. They focus on the life of sagacity—prudence, discipleship, a fence around the Torah. And, as we proceed, we find time and again that, while the word *Torah* stands for two things, divine revelation and the act of study of divine revelation, it produces a single effect, the transformation of unformed man into sage.

Clearly, tractate Abot explains the origins of the contents of the Mishnah, listing the Mishnah's authorities in the chain of tradition that began at Sinai. That explains why the document's focus rests not on Torah but on the life of sagacity (including, to be sure, Torah-study). But what defines and delimits Torah? It is the sage himself. So we may simply state the tractate's definition of Torah: Torah is what a sage learns. Accordingly, the Mishnah contains Torah. It may well be thought to fall into the classification of Torah. But the reason, we recognize, is that authorities whose sayings are found in the Mishnah possess Torah from Sinai. What they say, we cannot overemphasize, is Torah. How do we know it? It is a fact validated by the association of what they say with their own names. At issue in Abot is not the Torah, but the authority of the sage. It is that standing that transforms a saying into a Torah-saying, or to state matters more appropriately, that places a saying into the classification of the Torah. Abot then stands as the first document of the doctrine that the sage embodies the Torah and is a holy man, like Moses "our rabbi," in the likeness and image of God. The beginning is to claim that a saying falls into the category of Torah if a sage says it as Torah. The end will be to view the sage himself as Torah incarnate.

Beyond Abot, the Mishnah was joined by a great work of amplification and clarification of its law, called the Talmud of the Land of Israel (c. 400 C.E.). That document assigned to the Mishnah the same state as that of Scripture. And once the Mishnah entered the status of Scripture, it would take but a short step to a theory of the Mishnah as part of the revelation at Sinai—hence, oral Torah.

> R. Zeira in the name of R. Yohanan: "If a law comes to hand and you do not know its nature, do not discard it for another one, for lo, many laws were stated to Moses at Sinai, and all of them have been embedded in the Mishnah."
>
> —Yerushalmi Hagigah 1:7

The Mishnah now is claimed to contain statements made by God to Moses. Just how these statements found their way into the Mishnah, and which passages of the Mishnah contain them, we do not know. That is hardly important, given the fundamental assertion at hand. The passage proceeds to a further, and far more consequential, proposition. It asserts that part of the Torah was written down, and part was preserved in memory and transmitted orally. In context, moreover, that distinction must encompass the Mishnah, thus explaining its origin as part of the Torah. Here is a clear and unmistakable expression of the distinction between two forms in which a single Torah was revealed and handed on at Mount Sinai, part in writing, part orally. And, as we now see, the oral part of the Torah takes priority:

> R. Zeirah in the name of R. Eleazar: "'Were I to write for him my laws by ten thousands, they would be regarded as a strange thing' (Hosea 8:12). Now is the greater part of the Torah written down? [Surely not. The oral part is much greater.] But more abundant are the matters which are derived by exegesis from the written [Torah] than those derived by exegesis from the oral [Torah]."

And is that so?

But more cherished are those matters which rest upon the written [Torah] than those which rest upon the oral [Torah].

Haggai in the name of R. Samuel bar Nahman, "Some teachings were handed on orally, and some things were handed on in writing, and we do not know which of them is the more precious. But on the basis of that which is written, 'And the Lord said to Moses, Write these words; in accordance with these words I have made a covenant with you and with Israel' (Exodus 34:27), [we conclude] that the ones which are handed on orally are the more precious."

R. Yohanan and R. Yudan b. R. Simeon—One said, "If you have kept what is preserved orally and also kept what is in writing, I shall make a covenant with you, and if not, I shall not make a covenant with you.'"

The other said, "If you have kept what is preserved orally and you have kept what is preserved in writing, you shall receive a reward, and if not, you shall not receive a reward."

—Yerushalmi Hagigah 1:7

Here we have absolutely explicit evidence that people believed part of the Torah had been preserved not in writing but orally. Linking that part to the Mishnah remains a matter of implication. But it surely comes fairly close to the surface when we are told that the Mishnah contains Torah-traditions revealed at Sinai. From that view it requires only a small step to the allegation that the Mishnah is part of the Torah, the oral part.

The Torah as Source of Salvation

The single most consequential meaning assigned to "Torah" concerns salvation, inclusive of the miraculous. To define the category of the Torah as a source of salvation, as the Yerushalmi states matters, I point to a story that explicitly states the proposition that the Torah constitutes a source of salvation. In this story we shall see that because people observed the rules of the Torah, they expected to be saved. And if they did not observe, they accepted their punishment. So the Torah now stands for something more than revelation and a life of study, and (it goes without saying) the sage now appears as a holy, not merely a learned, man. This is because his knowledge of the Torah has transformed him. Accordingly, we deal with a category of stories and sayings about the Torah entirely different from what has gone before.

> As to Levi ben Sisi: troops came to his town. He took a scroll of the Torah and went up to the roof and said, "Lord of the ages! If a single word of this scroll of the Torah has been nullified [in our town], let them come up against us, and if not, let them go their way."
>
> Forthwith people went looking for the troops but did not find them [because they had gone their way].
>
> A disciple of his did the same thing, and his hand withered, but the troops went their way.
>
> A disciple of his disciple did the same thing. His hand did not wither, but they also did not go their way.
>
> This illustrates the following apophthegm: You can't insult an idiot, and dead skin does not feel the scalpel.
>
> —Y. Taanit 3:8

What is interesting here is how categories into which the word *Torah* previously fell have been absorbed and superseded in a new category altogether. The Torah is an object: "He took a scroll . . ." It also constitutes God's revelation to Israel: "If a single word . . ." The outcome of the revelation is to form an ongoing way of life, embodied in the sage himself: "A disciple of his did the same thing . . ." The sage plays an intimate part in the supernatural event: "His hand withered . . ." Now can we categorize this story as a statement that the Torah constitutes a particular object, or a source of divine revelation, or a way of life? Yes and no. The Torah here stands not only for the things we have already catalogued. It represents one more thing, which takes in all the others. Torah is a source of salvation. How so? The Torah stands for, or constitutes, the way in which the people Israel saves itself from marauders. This straightforward sense of salvation will not have surprised the author of Deuteronomy.

This new usage of the word *Torah* found in the Talmud of the Land of Israel emerges from a group of stories not readily classified in our established categories. All of these stories treat the word *Torah* (whether scroll, contents, or act of study) as source and guarantor of salvation. Accordingly, evoking the word *Torah* forms the centerpiece of a theory of Israel's history, on the one side, and an account of the teleology of the entire system, on the other. Torah indeed has ceased to constitute a specific thing or even a category or classification when stories about studying the Torah yield not a judgment as to status (i.e., praise for the learned man) but promise for supernatural blessing now and salvation in time to come.

To the rabbis the principal salvific deed was to "study Torah," by which they meant memorizing Torah-sayings by constant repetition, and, as the Talmud itself amply testifies (for some sages) profound analytic inquiry into the meaning of those sayings. The innovation now is that this act of "study of Torah" imparts supernatural power of a material character. For example, by repeating words of Torah, the sage could ward off the angel of death and accomplish other kinds of miracles as well. So Torah-formulas served as incantations. Mastery of Torah transformed the man engaged in Torah-learning into a supernatural figure, who could do things ordinary folk could not do. The category of "Torah" had already vastly expanded so that through transformation of the Torah from a concrete thing to a symbol, a Torah-scroll could be compared to a man of

Torah, namely, a rabbi. Now, once the principle had been established that salvation would come from keeping God's will in general, as Israelite holy men had insisted for so many centuries, it was a small step for rabbis to identify their particular corpus of learning—namely, the Mishnah and associated sayings—with God's will expressed in Scripture, the universally acknowledged medium of revelation.

The key to the Talmud's theory of the Torah lies in its conception of the sage, to which that theory is subordinate. Once the sage reaches his full apotheosis as Torah incarnate, then, but only then, the Torah becomes (also) a source of salvation in the present concrete formulation of the matter. That is why we traced the doctrine of the Torah in the salvific process by elaborate citation of stories about sages, living Torahs, exercising the supernatural power of the Torah, and serving, like the Torah itself, to reveal God's will. Since the sage embodied the Torah and gave the Torah, the Torah naturally came to stand for the principal source of Israel's salvation, not merely a scroll, on the one side, or a source of revelation, on the other.

WHAT ARE THE PRINCIPAL
SACRED TEXTS OF JUDAISM?
THE FORMS THEY TAKE

Among the many sacred texts of Judaism, two stand out: the Mishnah and the Midrash. The Mishnah is a single document, the Midrash, a whole collection of writings. The former is a law code, standing on its own. The latter is comprised of a set of exegeses, or amplifications, of books of Scripture. Let us deal with the Mishnah first.

The Mishnah

Falling into the hands of someone who has never seen it before, the Mishnah, whether in the Hebrew original or in English translation, must cause puzzlement. From the first line to the last, discourse takes up questions internal to a system that is never introduced. The Mishnah provides information without establishing context. It presents disputes about facts hardly urgent outside a circle of faceless disputants. Consequently, we start with the impression that we join a conversation already long under way about topics we can never grasp anyhow. Even though the language is our own, the substance is not. We shall feel as if we are in a transit lounge at a distant airport. We understand the words people say, but are baffled by their meanings and concerns, above all, by the urgency in their voices: What are you telling me? Why must I know it? Who cares if I do not?

No one can take for granted that what is before us makes sense in any context but the Mishnah's own, inaccessible world. The Mishnah in many tractates does not discuss topics of common interest. For before us is a remarkable statement of concerns for matters not only wholly remote from our own world, but, in the main, alien to the world of the people who made the Mishnah itself. It is as if people sat down to write letters about things they had never seen, to people they did not know—letters from an unknown city to an undefined and unimagined world: the Mishnah is a letter, written on blank paper, from no one special, located in utopia, to whom it may concern, at an indeterminate time and nowhere in particular. Perhaps its very power to speak from deep to deep is its lack of locative specificity. But internal evidence within the Mishnah certainly proves mute about all questions of authorship: where, when, why, for what purpose, to which audience? We know none of the answers to such basic questions as these.

Not only so, but, equally surprising, the Mishnah is a book without an author. Nowhere in its pages does the Mishnah identify its authors. It permits only slight variations, if any, in its authorities' patterns of language and speech, so there is no place for individual characteristics of expression. It nowhere tells us when it speaks. It does not address a particular place or time and rarely speaks of events in its own day. It never identifies its prospective audience. There is scarcely a "you" in the entire mass of sayings and rules. The Mishnah begins nowhere. It ends abruptly. There is no predicting where it will commence or explaining why it is done. Where, when, why the document is laid out and set forth are questions not deemed urgent and not answered.

Indeed, the Mishnah contains not a hint about what its authors conceive their work to be. Is it a law code? Is it a schoolbook? Since it makes statements describing what people should and should not do—or rather, do and do not do—we might suppose it is a law code. Since, as we shall see in a moment, it covers topics of both practical and theoretical interest, we might suppose it is a schoolbook. But the Mishnah never expresses a hint about its authors' intent. The reason is that the authors do what they must to efface all traces not only of individuality but even of their own participation in the formation of the document. So it is not only a letter from utopia to whom it may concern. It is also a letter written by no one person—but not by a committee either.

Nor should we fail to notice that while the Mishnah clearly addresses Israel, the Jewish people, it is remarkably indifferent to the Hebrew Scriptures. The Mishnah makes no effort at imitating the Hebrew of the Hebrew Bible, as do the writers of the Dead Sea Scrolls. The Mishnah does not attribute its sayings to biblical heroes, prophets, or holy men, as do the writings of the pseudepigraphs of the Hebrew Scriptures. The Mishnah does not claim to emerge from a fresh encounter with God through revelation, as is not uncommon in Israelite writings of the preceding four hundred years; the Holy Spirit is not alleged to speak here. So all the devices by which other Israelite writers gain credence for their messages are ignored. (We return to this puzzle in the chapter on Christianity.) Perhaps the authority of the Mishnah was self-evident to its authors. But, self-evident or not, they in no way take the trouble to explain to their document's audience why people should conform to the descriptive statements contained in their holy book.

If then we turn to the contents of the document, we are helped not at all in determining the place of the Mishnah's origination, the purpose of its formation, the reasons for its anonymous and collective plane of discourse and monotonous tone of voice. For the Mishnah covers a carefully defined program of topics. But the Mishnah never tells us why one topic is introduced and another is omitted, or what the agglutination of these particular topics is meant to accomplish in the formation of a system or imaginative construction. Nor is there any predicting how a given topic will be treated, why a given set of issues will be explored in close detail, and another set of possible issues ignored. Discourse on a theme begins and ends as if all things are self-evident—including, as I said, the reason for beginning at one point and ending at some other.

In all one might readily imagine, upon first glance at this strange and curious book, that what we have is a rulebook. It appears on the surface to be a book lacking all traces of eloquence and style, revealing no evidence of system and reflection, serving no important purpose. First glance indicates that what we have in hand is yet another sherd from remote antiquity—no different from the king lists inscribed on the ancient sherds, the random catalogue of (to us) useless, meaningless facts: a cookbook, a placard of posted tariffs, detritus of random information, accidentally thrown up on the currents of historical time. Who would want to have made such a thing? Who would now want to refer to it?

The answer to that question is deceptively straightforward. The Mishnah is important because it is a principal component of the canon of Judaism. Indeed, that answer begs the question: Why should some of the ancient Jews of the Holy Land have brought together these particular facts and rules into a book and set them forth for the Israelite people? Why should the Mishnah have been received, as much later on it certainly was received, as a half of the "whole Torah of Moses at Sinai"? The Mishnah was represented, after it was compiled, as the part of the "whole Torah of Moses, our rabbi," which had been formulated and transmitted orally, so it bore the status of divine revelation right alongside the Pentateuch. Yet it is already entirely obvious that little in the actual contents of the document evoked the character or the moral authority of the written Torah of Moses.

Indeed, since most of the authorities named in the Mishnah lived in the century and a half prior to the promulgation of the document, the claim that things said by men known to the very framers of the document in fact derived from Moses at Sinai through a long chain of oral tradition contradicted the well-known facts of the matter. So this claim presents a paradox even on the surface: How can the Mishnah be deemed a book of religion, a program for consecration, a mode of sanctification? Why should Jews from the end of the second century to our own day have deemed the study of the Mishnah to be a holy act, a deed of service to God through the study of an important constituent of God's Torah, God's will for Israel, the Jewish people?

In fact, the Mishnah is precisely that, a principal holy book of Judaism. The Mishnah has been and is now memorized in the circle of all those who participate in the religion of Judaism. Of still greater weight, the two great documents formed around the Mishnah and so shaped as to serve, in part, as commentaries to the Mishnah—namely, the Babylonian Talmud and the Palestinian Talmud—form the center of the curriculum of Judaism as a living religion. And all of this is present tense: the Mishnah, together with the Talmud and related writings, is studied and guides the life of Jews throughout the world, Reform, Orthodox, Conservative, Reconstructionist, and secular alike, in one way or another.

Let me now briefly describe the Mishnah. It is a six-part code of descriptive rules formed toward the end of the second century of the common era by a small number of Jewish sages and put forth as the constitution of Judaism under the sponsorship of Judah the Patriarch, the head of the Jewish community of the Land of Israel at the end of that century. The reason the document is important is that the Mishnah forms the foundation for the Babylonian and Palestinian Talmuds. It therefore stands alongside the Hebrew Bible as the holy book upon which the Judaism of the past nineteen hundred years is constructed. The six divisions are: (1) agricultural rules; (2) laws governing appointed seasons, e.g., Sabbaths and festivals; (3) laws on the transfer of women and property along with women from one man (father) to another (husband); (4) the system of civil and criminal law (corresponding to what we today should regard as "the legal system"); (5) laws for the conduct of the cult and the Temple; and (6) laws on the preservation of cultic purity both in the Temple and under certain domestic circumstances, with special reference to the table and bed. These divisions define the range and realm of reality.

When was the Mishnah made up, and who did the work? The world addressed by the Mishnah is hardly congruent to the worldview presented within the Mishnah. Let us now consider the time and context in which the document took shape. The Mishnah is made up of sayings bearing the names of authorities who lived, as I just said, in the later first century and the second century. (The book contains very little in the names of people who lived before the destruction of the Temple of Jerusalem in 70 C.E.) These authorities generally fall into two groups, namely, two distinct sets of names, each set of names randomly appearing together, but rarely, if ever, with names of the other set. The former set of names is generally supposed to represent authorities who lived between the destruction of the Temple in 70 and the advent of the second war against Rome, led by Simeon Bar Kokhba, in 132. The latter set of names belongs to authorities who flourished between the end of that war (c. 135) and the end of the second century.

The Mishnah itself is generally supposed to have come to closure at the end of the second century, and its date, for conventional purposes only, is c. 200 C.E. Now, of these two groups—sages from 70 to 130, and from 135 to 200—the latter is represented far more abundantly than the former. Approximately two-thirds of the named sayings belong to mid-second-century authorities. This is not surprising, since these are the named authorities whose (mainly unnamed) students collected, organized, and laid out the document as we now have it. So, in all, the Mishnah represents the thinking of Jewish sages who flourished in the middle of the second century. It is that group that took over whatever they had in hand from the preceding century—and from the whole legacy of Israelite literature even before that time—and revised and reshaped the whole into the Mishnah. Let us briefly consider their world, because the urgent question presented by that world precipitated the answer that, from then to now, Jews have found compelling as the reference point of their lives as a holy people.

In the aftermath of the war against Rome in 132–135, the Temple was declared permanently prohibited to Jews, and Jerusalem was closed off to them as well. So there was no cult, no Temple, no holy city, to which, at this time, the description of the Mishnaic laws applied. We observe at the very outset, therefore, that a sizable proportion of the Mishnah deals with matters to which the sages had no material access or practical knowledge at the time of their work. For we have seen that the Mishnah contains a division on the conduct of the cult, namely, the fifth, as well as one on the conduct of matters so as to preserve the cultic purity of the sacrificial system along the lines laid out in the book of Leviticus (the sixth division). In fact, a fair part of the second division, on appointed times, takes up the conduct of the cult on special days, e.g., the sacrifices offered on the Day of Atonement, Passover, and the like. Indeed, what the Mishnah wants to know about appointed seasons concerns the cult far more than it does the synagogue. The fourth division, on civil law, for its part, presents an elaborate account of a political structure and system of Israelite self-government, in tractates Sanhedrin and Makkot, not to mention Shebuot and Horayot. This system speaks of king, priest, Temple, and court. But it was not the Jews, their kings, priests, and judges, but the Romans who conducted the government of Israel in the Land of Israel in the time in which the second century authorities did their work.

So it would appear that well over half of the document before us speaks of cult, Temple, government, priesthood. As we shall see, moreover, the Mishnah takes up a profoundly priestly and Levitical conception of sanctification. When we consider that, in the very time in which the authorities before us did their work, the Temple lay in ruins, the city of Jerusalem was prohibited to all Israelites, and the Jewish government and administration that had centered on the Temple and based its authority on the holy life lived there were in ruins, the fantastic character of the Mishnah's address to its own catastrophic day becomes clear. Much of the Mishnah speaks of matters not in being in the time in which the Mishnah was created, because the Mishnah wishes to make its statement on what really matters.

In the age beyond catastrophe, the problem is to reorder a world off course and adrift, to gain reorientation for an age in which the sun has come out after the night and the fog. The Mishnah is a document of imagination and fantasy, describing how things "are" out of the sherds and remnants of reality, but, in larger measure, building social being out of beams of hope. The Mishnah tells us something about how things were, but everything about how a small group of men wanted things to be. The document is orderly, repetitious, careful in both language and message. It is small-minded, picayune, obvious, dull, routine—everything its age was not. The Mishnah stands in contrast with the world to which it speaks. Its message is one of small achievements and modest hope. It means to defy a world of large disorders and immodest demands. The heirs of heroes build an unheroic folk in the new and ordinary age. The Mishnah's message is that what a person wants matters in important ways. It states that message to an Israelite world that can shape affairs in no important ways and speaks to people who by no means will the way things now are. The Mishnah therefore lays down a practical judgment upon, and in favor of, the imagination and will to reshape reality, regain a system, reestablish that order upon which trustworthy existence is to be built.

The Mishnah's mode of speech—the way it speaks, not only what it says—is testimony to its highest and most enduring, distinctive value. Now let us take note. This language does not speak of sacred symbols but of pots and pans, of menstruation and dead creeping things, of ordinary water which, because of the circumstance of its collection and location, possesses extraordinary power; of the commonplace corpse and ubiquitous diseased person; of genitalia and excrement, toilet seats and the flux of penises, of stems of pomegranates and stalks of leeks; of rain and earth and wood, metal, glass, and hide. This language is filled with words for neutral things of humble existence. It does not speak of holy things and is not symbolic in its substance. This language speaks of ordinary things, of things that everyone must have known. But because of the peculiar and particular way in which it is formed and formalized, this same language not only adheres to an aesthetic theory but expresses a deeply embedded ontology and methodology of the sacred, specifically of the sacred within the secular, and of the capacity for regulation, therefore for sanctification, within the ordinary: All things in order, all things then hallowed by God who orders all things, so said the priests' creation tale. The Mishnah is the other side of creation: a picture of that well-ordered, stable world that God called God, blessed, and sanctified. And, in its odd and strange portrait of a utopian never-never land, the Mishnah told Israel, the Jewish people, about that basic structure of life in society that, wherever Israel made its home, the holy people of God would comprise.

The Midrash

Judaism is a religion that moves forward by looking backward. That is to say, by constantly sifting and resifting the Torah, the sages made sense of their own times and explained the meaning of events. Hence the study of Scripture, the clarification and amplification of its words—this work of exegesis called Midrash formed the principal activity in the disposition of sacred texts. It is no exaggeration to say that the history of Judaism is the exegesis of exegesis: the explanation of the Judaic encounter with the Torah.

Three components join together to make possible the work of Midrash: the received text of the written Torah; the person of the sage, master of the Torah; and events or issues of the present age. The power of the sage lay in his ability to interpret events and settle issues by appeal to the received Torah, and the dynamism of the process derived from the interplay of the sage and the critical concerns of the moment. The exegesis of verses of Scripture defined a convention in Israelite life even before books of holy writings attained the status of Scripture. The relationship of Chronicles to Samuel and Kings shows us how, within the life of ancient Israel, people read one book in the light of events of a later age, imposing an issue important to themselves upon writings of the remote past. Every known Judaism in ancient times, whether revealed in the writings of a sect, such as at Qumran among the Essenes, or in those of a philosopher, such as Philo, undertook to interpret verses of

Scripture as part of the labor of defining the Judaism at hand, its worldview and way of life.

There are three types of Midrash-writing that we find in the Torah. In the first, the focus of interest is on individual verses of Scripture, and interpreting those verses, in the sequence in which they appear, forms the organizing principle of sustained discourse. In the second, the center of interest attends to the testing and validating of large-scale propositions, which, through the reading of individual verses, an authorship wishes to test and validate. In that rather philosophical trend in rabbinic Bible interpretation, the interpretation of individual verses takes a subordinated position, the appeal to facts of Scripture in the service of the syllogism at hand. The third approach directs attention not to concrete statements of Scripture, whether in sequences of verses or merely individual verses or even words or phrases, but to entire compositions of Scripture: biblical themes, stories. This investigation of Scripture's meaning generates Midrash as narrative: the imaginative recasting of Scripture's stories in such a way as to make new and urgent points through the retelling.

The single striking trait of Midrash as produced by the Judaism of the dual Torah is the persistent appeal, in interpreting a verse or a theme of Scripture, to some other set of values or considerations than those contained within the verse or topic at hand. On that account I classify rabbinic Midrash as parabolic or allegorical, in the sense that it compares something to something else, as does a parable, or it explains something in terms of something else, as does allegory. But these terms are used not in a technical sense but only in the most general way. Rabbinic Midrash reads Scripture within the principle that things never are what they seem. At the foundations of the hermeneutical pretense lies the long-standing biblical-Jewish insistence that Israel's sorry condition in no way testifies to Israel's true worth—the grandest pretense of all. All of the little evasions of the primary sense in favor of some other testify to this, the great denial that what is, is what counts. Midrash in the Judaism of the dual Torah makes that statement with art and imagination. But it is never subtle about saying so.

Through Midrash, the rabbinic sages mediated between Israel's perceived condition in an uncertain world and Israel's vivid faith in the God who chooses Israel and reveals the Torah. Faced with an unredeemed world, sages read Scripture as an account of how things are meant to be. To them, things are not what they seem, and that was a judgment made not only about this world but also about Scripture. This world does not testify to God's wish and plan, and Scripture does not record merely the stories and sayings that we read there. This world serves as a metaphor for Scripture's reality, and Scripture provides a metaphor for Israel's as well. Reading one thing in terms of something else, the rabbinic exegetes produced in Midrash a powerful instrument of theological renewal through Scripture.

A single trait of mind characterized all rabbinic Midrash-processes or hermeneutics and therefore all rabbinic Midrash-exegesis and, further, explained the purpose and plan of all rabbinic Midrash-compilations. It was the Midrash-process that lay at the heart of matters, specifically, the premise by which, as a rabbinic exegete read a scriptural text, that exegete would read matters. To state the matter simply: rabbinic Midrash-process produced Midrash-exegeses that came together in Midrash-compilations in order to spell out how one thing stood for something else, that is, that fundamentally parabolic reading of Scripture that presents one of the three principal alternatives of Midrash that late antiquity shows us. What happens in Midrash in the Judaism of the dual Torah?

The verses that are quoted in rabbinic Midrash ordinarily shift from the meanings they convey to the implications they contain, so speaking about something, anything, other than what they seem to be saying. The as-if frame of mind brought to

Scripture renews Scripture, with the sage seeing everything with fresh eyes. And the result of the new vision was a reimagining of the social world envisioned by the document at hand, I mean, the everyday world of Israel in its Land in that difficult time. For what the sages now proposed was a reconstruction of existence along the lines of the ancient design of Scripture as they read it. What that meant was that, from a sequence of one-time and linear events, everything that happened was turned into a repetition of known and already experienced paradigms, hence, once more, a mythic being. The source and core of the myth, of course, derive from Scripture—Scripture reread, renewed, reconstructed along with the society that revered Scripture.

Reading one thing in terms of something else, the builders of the document systematically adopted for themselves the reality of the Scripture, its history and doctrines. They transformed that history from a sequence of one-time events, leading from one place to some other, into an ever-present mythic world. No longer was there one Moses, one David, one set of happenings of a distinctive and never-to-be-repeated character. Now whatever happened of which the thinkers propose to take account must enter and be absorbed into that established and ubiquitous pattern and structure founded in Scripture. It is not that biblical history repeats itself. Rather, biblical history no longer constitutes history as a story of things that happened once, long ago, and pointed to some one moment in the future. Rather it becomes an account of things that happen every day—hence, an ever-present mythic world, as I said. That is why, in Midrash in the Judaism of the dual Torah, Scripture as a whole does not dictate the order of discourse, let alone its character. In this document they chose a verse here, a phrase there. In the more mature Midrash-compilations, such as Leviticus Rabbah and Pesiqta deRab Kahana, these then presented the pretext for propositional discourse commonly quite out of phase with the cited passage.

The framers of the Midrash-documents saw Scripture in a new way, just as they saw their own circumstance afresh. Specifically, they rejected their world in favor of Scripture's, reliving Scripture's world in their own terms. That, incidentally, is why they did not write history, an account of what was happening and what it meant. It was not that they did not recognize or appreciate important changes and trends reshaping their nation's life. They could not deny that reality. In their apocalyptic reading of the dietary and leprosy laws, as we shall see in Leviticus Rabbah, they made explicit their close encounter with the history of the world as they knew it. But they had another mode of responding to history. It was to treat history as if it were already known and readily understood. Whatever happened had already happened. Scripture dictated the contents of history, laying forth the structures of time, the rules that prevailed and were made known in events. Self-evidently, these same thinkers projected into Scripture's day the realities of their own, turning Moses and David into rabbis, for example. But that is how people think in that mythic, enchanted world in which, to begin with, reality blends with dream, and hope projects onto future and past alike how people want things to be. No wonder, then, that we may write the history of Judaism as the exegesis of exegesis!

LITURGICAL, INTELLECTUAL, POLITICAL, AND RITUAL USES OF SACRED TEXTS

Enough has been said about the Mishnah and Midrash to leave no doubt about the intellectual and political uses of the Torah. But what about the Torah in liturgy and rite?

In the synagogue services on the Sabbath, as well as on Mondays and on Thursdays, the Torah is read with great precision and solemnity. At that moment, the Torah is received as if from Sinai. The Torah—now the Torah-scrolls, containing the Five Books of Moses—stands at the center of Judaic worship.

The liturgy of the synagogue itself insists that the synagogue rite of proclaiming the Torah forms a moment of revelation: God giving the Torah. The language of the blessings recited before and after the reading of a Torah-lection says precisely that. The blessing speaks of the here and now, using as it does the present tense: "blessed . . . who gives the Torah." That refers to what happens here and now, in fact and in effect, just as the blessing for bread, "who brings forth bread to the earth," speaks of what happens in the here and now. Other blessings using the perfect tense, "who has kept us in life, has sustained us, and has brought us to this season," show that the tense represents a matter of choice. Furthermore, even the blessing over the Torah fore and aft mixes tenses: "who has chosen us from all peoples and has given us the Torah . . . blessed . . . who gives," and at the end, "who has given us the Torah of truth and planted in our midst eternal life," and, then again, ". . . who gives." The election took place in the beginning and endures; the Torah marked and marks the election. Through the authentic Torah eternal life has taken root among us. These statements reach far into the distant, governing past: time gone. But they speak to the present, especially to the present: ". . . who gives . . ."

The choice of present tense is deliberate, It serves to say that Sinai is not a place nor a merely one-time, past-time historical event. It is a moment of eternity, when the eternal breaks into time and shatters one-time history with timeless truth: reliable mathematics replicates nature's uncertain processes. It is an hour beyond time marked specifically by what happens whenever in the holy community of the faithful the Torah is removed from the holy ark, danced with and paraded, displayed, read, opened full breadth to the community to inspect, paraded again and reverently returned to its ark. That is what "giving the Torah" and "receiving of the Torah" by God and Israel, respectively, or, in theological language, what "revelation," means. And in the synagogue and academy that is not an act of commemoration or even replication but—once more I stress—of re-presentation. When the Torah is given, then we are, we become, Israel; there we know God.

For the giving of the Torah—in secular language, revelation—to take place what is required is not place but identification of place, not just persons whom it may concern, but the holy people. The right people, at the right time, with the right attitude receive the Torah, and what they do at such a time in such a place furthermore defines what it means for Israel to receive the Torah. In this context "situation" speaks of circumstance, not location: God comes through the Torah to Israel, which is a utopian, not a locative category. And God comes not promiscuously but in measured moments: at the time of finding, when in the Torah God wishes to be found. The circumstance of saying "blessed . . . who gives the Torah," or reciting at the end, "Magnified and sanctified be the great name in the world that he created in accord with his will," defines the conditions of giving and receiving the Torah, that is, the act and moment of revelation.

We note the implacably public character of the event. The religious encounter afforded by the Torah takes principal place not for the private person but in public, in a moment of community and of communion: Israel with Israel, Israel with God. The act consists in the shared act and moment of hearing and receiving the gift of the Torah. The gift has to be received, accepted, acknowledged, and, in the nature of the holy life of Israel, that means, by Israel as a whole, as at Sinai. The unacknowledged gift is an insult. How is this shared acknowledgement, this public engagement with the gift, to be accomplished? The Torah not only reveals that God is, but what God says and wants: propositions. And it follows, the way in which Israel receives the gift of the Torah is through its understanding, its capacity to persuade itself in all rationality to affirm and obey. That is why in the synagogue the Torah is not only displayed but read. That fact further explains why in the academy the Torah is not only read but analyzed. It is in the life of the mind that Israel receives the gift, that Judaism affirms revelation. The rigorous composition of theology then forms the counterpart, in secular language, to the act of rational affirmation, in the language of the Torah: we shall do and we shall obey. And that fact brings us back once again to the center of matters, the public and communal quality of the meeting with God and leads us to understand why we must understand the Torah as God's song. There is nothing so public, and that by definition, as intellect.

That assembly takes place on Sabbath after Sabbath when Israel is assembled, as at Sinai, to celebrate the Torah by paying attention to it and so asserting who Israel too is, as the blessing before the Torah states: "Blessed are you, Lord, our God, ruler of the world, who has chosen us from among all the peoples by having given us the Torah. Blessed are you, who gives the Torah." At the end come similar words, referring to us, Israel: "who has given us the Torah that is true and planted within us eternal life." So much for individuals in families assembled in the synagogue: chosen through the Torah. They form Israel, celebrate and study the Torah, and so meet God.

CHAPTER 2

Islam

HOW DOES ISLAM MAKE ITS ENDURING STATEMENTS? WHAT DOES ISLAM MEAN BY A TEXT?

Islam understands all authority to rest in God, who has communicated the divine message to humankind through three sacred texts, the Torah, the Gospel, and the Qur'ān . But while it is correct to say that the only sacred text in Islam is the Qur'ān (since the first two texts are understood to have been corrupted), this is not an adequate account of the way Islam has made its enduring statements. For a full theory of sacred text and authority, we must turn to the writings of early Islamic scholars, who struggled to develop a workable theory of law and ethics for the new religion.

The first theoretical explanation of authority was written by Muḥammad b. Idrīs al-Shāfi'ī, who died in 820 C.E. in Egypt, almost 200 years after the death of the Prophet. In his *al-Risāla fī uṣūl al-fiqh* (*Treatise on the Foundations of Jurisprudence*), commonly known simply as the *Risāla*, al-Shāfi'ī argued a descending order of authority in Islam, beginning with the Qur'ān, but followed by the *sunna* of the Prophet (his "general way of doing things") and thirdly by human reason. Al-Shāfi'ī's system was controversial at first. In fact, the full implications for orthodox religious thought were not fully worked out until the time of Abū Ḥāmid al-Ghazzālī (d. IIII in Ṭūs). Ultimately, though, this tripartite system (of Qur'ān, sunna, and reason) dominated, even among Sufi and Shī'ite heterodoxies.

Al-Shāfi'ī wrote his *Risāla* during a turbulent time, when the Islamic empire had reached its largest extent, from the Atlantic coast of Africa to the mountains of the Indian subcontinent, and a centralized bureaucracy was developing in the new city of Baghdad. Yet with all this wealth and influence, the empire was being split by divisive battles over doctrine. Every main city of the empire—Fusṭāṭ, Mecca, Medina, Damascus, Basra, and Kufa—had its own schools of Islamic law, its own tradition, and even its own way of reading the Qur'ān. Since al-Shāfi'ī was born in Palestine, studied in Medina, and lived in Iraq and Egypt, he knew something of these regional loyalties and was in a unique position to strike a balance between the main rivals in Kufa and Medina. His theory of authority, though never accepted in his lifetime, would help define the Prophet's sunna as a sacred text; at the same time it enshrined the authority of the 'ulamā', the "people of knowledge." He wrote:

> The sum-total of what God has declared to His creatures in His book, by which He invited them to worship Him in accordance with His prior decision, includes various categories. One of these is what He has declared to His creatures by texts [in the Qur'ān], such as the aggregate of duties owing to Him: That they shall perform the prayer, pay the alms tax, perform the pilgrimage, and observe the fast. And that He has forbidden disgraceful acts—both visible and hidden—and in the textual prohibition of adultery, the drinking of wine, eating the flesh of dead things and of blood and pork; and He has made clear to them how to perform the duty of the major ablution as well as other matters stated precisely in the text of the Qur'ān.
>
> A second category consists of those duties the obligation of which He established in His Book, but the modes of which He made clear by the tongue of His Prophet. The number of prayers

each day and the amount of alms tax and their time of fulfillment are cases in point; but there are other similar duties which He has revealed in His Book.

A third category consists of that which the Apostle of God established by example or exhortation, but in regard to which there is no precisely defined rule from God [in the Qur'ān]. For God has laid down in His Book the obligation of obedience to His apostle and recourse to his decision. So he who accepts a duty on the authority of the Apostle of God accepts it by the obligation imposed by God.

A fourth category consists of what God commanded His creatures to seek through personal reasoning.

—al-Shāfiʿī, *Risāla*, 67–68[1]

Al-Shāfiʿī's delineation of categories is important on a number of levels. First, while he says in the first sentence that all authoritative statements are to be found in "His book," the third and fourth categories are no longer based on Qur'ān. Rather, the Prophet's sunna gains second place, and human reason is a source of authority in its own right.

On a second level, al-Shāfiʿī has sacrificed the authority of the rival schools of law in favor of his threefold system. While no Muslim was likely to challenge the primacy of Qur'ān or sunna in *theory,* in practice the Qur'ān only has about 600 verses with clear directives to believers on ethics, ritual, and law. Neither were there Prophetic sunna regarding every situation. As a result, religious scholars before al-Shāfiʿī based their interpretation of Islamic doctrine on other sources, including old Arab custom and local practice.

For instance, when al-Shāfiʿī's own teacher, Mālik b. Anas (d. 795 in Medina), sought to provide a rule on the Islamic way to emancipate slaves, he struggled with a Qur'ānic verse on the subject, but ultimately abandoned this verse in favor of local practice. In the Sura of Light, the Qur'ān reads: "As for those slaves who request a contract of emancipation from you, contract with them if you know some good in them" (24:33). This was not, Mālik argued, a command from God that all slaves who asked for emancipation must automatically receive it; rather it is more like a suggestion from God. As evidence for this interpretation, however, he turned to the living tradition of Medina, the Prophet's own city, reasoning that whatever local customs the Prophet did not explicitly reject, he must have accepted. Note the claims to authority made by Mālik in this passage.

> Mālik said: According to *our way*, it is not incumbent upon the master of a slave to enter into an emancipation contract with his slave if the slave requests this of him. *I have not heard that any religious leader* ever forced a man to enter into an emancipation contract with his slave. *I have heard that one of the Learned*, when asked about this and told that God—blessed and exalted is He—said: "Enter into an emancipation contract with them if you know some good in them!" (24:33), recited two Qur'ān verses: "When you are free of the state of ritual purity, then hunt!" (5:3) and "When the prayer is finished scatter in the land and seek God's bounty!" (62:10). Mālik said: Surely this is a matter which God, mighty and exalted is He, has permitted the people; it is not a duty upon them.
>
> —Mālik, *Muwaṭṭa'*, 2:147–48[2]

Mālik opens his argument by stating the local consensus of Medina ("our way"), asserting that he had never heard anyone promote the contrary opinion. While this is a strong argument, it is not based on the Qur'ān. He then continues by quoting an anonymous authority who cleverly juxtaposes two other Qur'ān verses with this verse, arguing that they only appear to be commands. In the ensuing discussion of this emancipation contract, Mālik explains another Qur'ān verse in the same way, assuring the reader that this exegesis conforms to "common practice." He then includes some random notes on the subject from two companions of the Prophet: 'Abd Allāh b. 'Umar and 'Uthmān b. 'Affān.

> Mālik said: I heard one of the Learned saying about God's word— blessed and exalted is He: "Give them of the wealth of God which He has given you" (24:33) that it meant that when a man enters into an emancipation contract with his male slave, he should re- duce the slave's burden by granting him a designated amount at the end of his contract. Mālik continued: This is what I have heard from the Learned; I have noted that this is the common practice of our people.
>
> Mālik said: It has come to my attention that 'Abd Allāh b. 'Umar entered into a contract with one of his male slaves for 35,000 dirhams and then reduced the end of the slave's contract by 5,000 dirhams.
>
> —Mālik, *Muwaṭṭa'*, 2:148

> Mālik reported to us on the authority of his uncle Abū Suhayl b. Mālik, whose father heard 'Uthmān b. 'Affān while he was preach- ing and saying: Do not demand a wage from the female slave who has no particular skill, for surely when you demand this of her, she will earn her wage through prostitution.
>
> —Mālik, *Muwaṭṭa'*, 2:278–79

In this passage, Mālik uses the Qur'ān as one voice of authority among several others. Further, the authoritative stories used to explain this point do not come from the Prophet, but from his companions. Therefore, Mālik's students would find them- selves hard-pressed to follow al-Shāfiʿī's new rules, especially when Qur'ān verses are ambiguous and no Prophetic hadith (*ḥadīth*) are available. Some of Mālik's students went so far as to write legal treatises which seemed to place personal opinion and local custom in a position of greater authority than that of the Prophet. With this type of opposition, al-Shāfiʿī had to develop sound arguments to convince his readers of the need to raise the Prophet's sunna to the level of binding law. In the following passage, he addresses his opposition directly, marshalling evidence from the Qurʾān itself to put the Prophet in place as a source for sacred authority.

> As far as faith, duty, and the Qurʾān are concerned, God placed his Messenger in such a position that would make it obvious that God made him knowledgeable over his religion. This is made clear in God's imposition of obedience to him, his prohibition of disobedience to him, and his making the Prophet's virtues obvious. It is also made clear in that God has connected belief in his Messenger with belief in him. For God—blessed and exalted is he—said: "Believe in God and his messengers, and do not say: [God is] three. Cease; it will be better for you. God is only one God. Glory be to him, that he should have a son" (4:169).
>
> He also said: "Surely it is those who have believed in God and his Messenger who are the believers, and those who, when they are with him on some common affair, do not go away until they ask his permission" (24:62).
>
> In this way, God laid down the perfect beginning of the faith, after which all other things follow: belief in God and then in his Messenger. For if a servant believes only in him, not in his Messenger, the name of the perfect faith (i.e., Islam) will never settle upon him, unless he believes in his Messenger along with him.
>
> —al-Shāfiʿī, *Risāla*, 73–75[3]

Again, few could argue with al-Shāfiʿī the importance of Muḥammad as the recipient of revelation, but as a practical source of guidance, the Prophet's sunna seemed weak. Not only were there no statements (hadith) by the Prophet on various important issues, but the process of transmitting his hadith over generations also resulted in false ascriptions, contradictions, and even open fabrications. Al-Shāfiʿī was well aware of these problems but only proposed a rough solution, suggesting that correct sunna could be tested against the Qurʾān or against other sunna.

> The contradictory Sunna is due to incomplete transmission rendering it contradictory, as I have explained before, although what was lacking can be known from other traditions, or it is the product of the transmitter's imagination. No contradictory tradition from the Prophet is known to us for which a possible explanation is lacking.
>
> —al-Shāfiʿī, *Risāla*, 182

Al-Shāfiʿī's argument demonstrates that he is more interested in asserting the validity of hadith than in providing a workable system, and even al-Shāfiʿī's own followers did not implement his theory of authority in every case. Al-Shāfiʿī's theories had a long way to go before being fully accepted.

In order to facilitate the use of Prophetic sunna as an authoritative source, scholars in the generation after al-Shāfiʿī began to collect and organize individual hadiths, either according to the recognized chapters of Islamic law (moving from prayer to pilgrimage on through to rules on marriage and business transactions) or on the basis of the names of the persons who transmitted them. These first collections were small, incorporating only a few thousand hadith. Quickly, however, they grew to include tens of thousands of hadith. The reason for this explosion in Prophetic hadith in the ninth and tenth centuries is a source of great controversy, and while it is possible that some new hadith were found, it is clear that many rulings that were formerly based on custom and local practice now appear as actual hadith of the Prophet. Quite simply, once the thesis of authority resting in the words of the Prophet had been advanced, it could not be reversed, and all Muslim scholars eventually conformed to this rule. By the eleventh century, a consensus regarding religious authority in Islam had been recorded by one of Islam's greatest theologians, who was also a follower of al-Shāfiʿī's school, Abū Ḥāmid al-Ghazzālī (d. 1111):

> The foundations of the religious law are four: (1) the book of God, (2) the sunna of God's messenger, and (3) the consensus of the religious leaders and the traditions of the companions of the Prophet. As for this consensus, it is a foundation to the extent that it directs one to the sunna, for it is a foundation of the third rank. The statements of the companions are similar, for they also direct one to the sunna. After all, the companions witnessed the inspiration of and revelation to the Prophet and they comprehended the clear meanings of the revelation due to their knowledge of its relationship to particular circumstances, which were concealed from others. It is possible that the obvious expression of the revelation does not encompass that which was obvious at the time. (4) Along these lines, the opinion of the exemplary scholars may also be seen as a foundation of the religious law, along with their traditions, although this is with special conditions, particularly regarding the person who gives the opinion, although the elucidation of these restrictions is not fitting in these pages.
>
> —al-Ghazzālī, *Iḥya*, 1:27–28[4]

With all this focus on the importance of the Qur'ān and sunna as sources for religious authority in Islam, one should not lose sight of al-Shāfiʿī's category of human reason. In this passage, al-Ghazzālī has restricted the use of human reason to the specific task of interpreting Qur'ān and sunna and the opinions of past scholars. Nevertheless, individual reasoning continues to play a large role in Islam, particularly due to decentralization of religious authority. It is important to remember that Islamic law is not a defined code, with clear rules and prescribed punishments. It is, rather, a process of divining God's will in a particular situation. In a Muslim court of law, this means that every case is treated individually, with the judge using his reason to apply the sources to each new situation. But while in the field of orthodox jurisprudence authority was thought to rest primarily in Qur'ān, then sunna, then consensus of the scholars, and finally in personal opinion, heterodox movements located authority in other quarters.

In Shī'ism, for instance, the authority of the Prophet extends primarily to the rest of his family. Therefore, the union of his daughter Fāṭima and his son-in-law 'Alī is of central importance, since their descendants are understood to have a special ability to interpret the Qur'ān and even provide a continuation of revelation. The largest group of Shī'ites today are known as "twelvers" due to their belief that the twelfth descendent of the Prophet, Muḥammad al-Mahdī, went into a state of occultation at the end of the ninth century. From that point on, certain persons were understood to maintain contact with this "twelfth Imam," providing guidance for his community in his absence; this Imam is to return at the end of time to establish a reign of justice. In Shī'ism, therefore, the authority of this Imam, and those who speak for him, provides a variation on the rules established in orthodox Islam (Sunnism).

Shī'ites use the same Qur'ān as that used by Sunnites, and though they also use many of the same hadith, they prefer hadith transmitted by members of the Prophet's family as being more trustworthy. While these slight differences lead to variations in interpretation of religious law, Shī'ites and Sunnites share many of the same rituals and practices. Within the community, however, twelver Shī'ites have a more unified practice than do Sunnites. This unity derives from a developed sense of clergy among Shī'ites, with a specific hierarchy of authority, leading up to one or more persons, known as *marja'-i taqlīd*, or "source of imitation." Principle Shī'ite countries today are Iran,

Yemen, Iraq, and Bahrain, with significant populations in India, Pakistan, and Lebanon.

While Sufism, Islamic mysticism, cannot be called a heterodox movement in the same way as Shī'ism, the relative orthodoxy of various Sufi groups can be determined by the extent to which they follow Sunnite theories of sacred authority. One Sufi maxim declares *sharī'a, ṭarīqa, ḥaqīqa* ("divine law, mystical path, divine reality") as the epitome of the Sufi quest. Such a formulation valorizes the system of religious authority established by al-Shāfi'ī as the necessary foundation for the search for divine truth. It also suggests that sharī'a is but a first step toward that "divine reality" that can only be realized by pursuing the mystical path. Depending on the particular group, this path consists of commitments to service, asceticism, and/or meditation.

Other forms of Sufism leave orthodoxy behind, asserting a radical unity with God, and even with all creation. These movements on the edge of Islam locate authority primarily in a teacher, or even in an idealized version of Muḥammad or 'Alī as "The Perfect Man." For these extremists, Qur'ān and religious law in general can be seen as a trap, which veils the truth from the believer. Even al-Ghazzālī, the most orthodox of mystics, is sensitive to this criticism, urging his readers to avoid following a single school of interpretation in a dogmatic fashion. Rather, the believer should use spiritual insight to interpret the text. On the other hand, al-Ghazzālī actively encourages study of the text and its various interpretations, which some see as a mere veil around mystical insight. He writes, "As for true knowledge which is actually the uncovering and the seeing of the truth by the light of spiritual insight, how can it be a veil, since it is the ultimate object of desire?" (al-Ghazzālī, *Iḥyā*, 1: 335). In this question, al-Ghazzālī lands the believer back where al-Shāfi'ī started: the relationship of human reason with the sacred texts. As impressive an authority as the Qur'ān is, being God's direct speech, religious authority must reside in a broader world, primarily in the words and deeds of God's Prophet, but also in the fallible human creatures who must use their reason to interpret and apply God's commands.

This interplay of reason and revelation helps explain Islam's view of text, for text is principally the spoken, not the written, word. For a full understanding of the Qur'ān, it must be conceived as the word of God *spoken* to Muḥammad, just as Muslims believe that God revealed his book to Moses and Jesus. The Prophet is then also seen as living text, as an example to humankind by virtue of his words and deeds. Finally, all those who imitate the Prophet, be they Sufi saints or Shī'ite Imams, can be seen as living texts, and through this process, their spoken words also have authority.

WHAT ARE THE PRINCIPAL
SACRED TEXTS OF ISLAM?
THE FORMS THEY TAKE

From the above discussion, it is clear that the two principle sacred texts that all Muslims see as authoritative are the Qur'ān and the sunna of the Prophet. Importantly, these two texts take on very different forms. The Qur'ān is a fixed text and was compiled within a few decades of the Prophet's death (traditionally by the Caliph 'Uthmān b. 'Affān in 650 C.E.). While the Muslim tradition records hundreds of variant readings for the Qur'ān, these variations rarely have a significant impact on the meaning of the text. Over time, a single version, without variants, has become accepted by the majority of Muslims. The sunna of the Prophet, however, has never been reduced to a single authoritative collection, and Muslims continue to publish eclectic compilations of the Prophet's hadith.

The Qur'ān is a substantial book, but not a large one, being shorter than both the Hebrew and Christian scriptures. Unlike these books, it contains no historical accounts, either of Muhammad or of the early community. In fact, it is impossible to determine the historical order of the 114 suras (chapters) that make up the Qur'ān, though various rough categories have been attempted. Such a lack of internal chronological coherence has opened the door to speculation that the Qur'ān may not have been compiled in 650 after all, but perhaps decades later. In general, however, both Muslim and non-Muslim scholars accept the traditional account of compilation.

According to this account, the Qur'ān was revealed over the last two decades of Muḥammad's lifetime, from the beginning of his mission around the year 610 in his home city of Mecca, to his death in 632 in Medina. To understand the place of both Qur'ān and sunna in Islam, one must recount the story of Muḥammad's mission, one of the central myths of Islam. The famous historian Abū Ja'far al-Ṭabarī (d. 923) recorded this account of God's call to Muḥammad in the month of Ramadan:

> The Messenger of God went out as usual to the cave of Ḥirā' accompanied by his family. When the night came, on which God ennobled him by making him his Messenger and thereby showed mercy to his servants, Gabriel brought him the command of God.
>
> The Messenger of God said, "Gabriel came to me as I was sleeping with a brocade cloth in which was some writing. He said, "Recite!" and I said, "I cannot recite." He pressed me tight and almost stifled me, until I thought that I should die. Then he let me go, and said, "Recite!" I said, "What shall I recite?" only saying that in order to free myself from him, fearing that he might repeat what he had done to me. He said:
>> Recite in the name of thy Lord who creates!
>> He creates man from a clot of blood.
>> Recite: And your Lord is the Most Bountiful,
>> He who teaches by the pen,
>> Teaches man what he knew not. (96:1–5)

I recited it, and then he desisted and departed. I woke up, and it
was as though these words had been written on my heart.

—al-Ṭabarī, *History*, 71[5]

As the account continues, it becomes clear that Muḥammad
did not know what to do with this new designation as a messenger of God; he is shown as being uncertain of his mission,
and even his sanity. According to some accounts, it was Khadīja, his wife, who would determine that he was being visited
by an angel and not a devil. It would also be three years before
he would begin preaching openly his message of repentance
and reform to his fellow Meccans. The earliest suras of the
Qur'ān are full of these exhortations: short, pithy prophetic utterances found in the rhymed prose (*saj'*) used by Arabian ora-
cles and soothsayers.

In the Name of God, the Merciful, the Compassionate

By Heaven and the night-star!
And what shall teach thee what is the night-star?
The piercing star!
Over every soul there is a watcher.

So let man consider of what he was created;
he was created of gushing water
issuing between the loins and the breast-bones.
Surely He is able to bring him back
upon the day when the secrets are tried,
and he shall have no strength, no helper.

By heaven of the returning rain,
by earth splitting with verdure,
surely it is a decisive word;
it is no merriment.

> They are devising guile,
> and I am devising guile.
> So respite the unbelievers; delay with them awhile.
>
> —The Night Star. 86:1–17

This is the entire 86th sura, and it is typical of the early message of the Qur'ān. In these passages, the Qur'ān is addressed specifically to the polytheist Meccans, trying to convince them of God's position as creator and sustainer. From the outset, the Qur'ān speaks with the voice of God, hinting at secrets of creation and his role as sustainer of the world, as well as of "the day when secrets are tried" at the end of time. Also, as is usual in the Qur'ān, God speaks in multiple voices, here both in first-person singular ("I am devising guile") and in third-person singular ("He is able to bring him back"); first-person plural is also often used.

When Muḥammad first began to preach in the streets of Mecca, his message was seen as being within the bounds of the worship of many gods and goddesses at the central shrine, the *Ka'ba*. The Meccan cult of worship at the Ka'ba was the source of both pride and economic stability in Mecca, as rules were set up to restrict inter-tribal feuds in the holy precinct, making Mecca a safe haven for trade. Suras of this period invoke the example of past prophets, fitting well into Meccan eclecticism; for instance, this sura speaks first of Noah and the great flood:

> The people of Noah cried lies before them;
> they cried lies to Our servant, and said,
> "A man possessed!" And he was rejected.
> And so he called unto his Lord, saying,
> "I am vanquished; do Thou succour me!"
> Then We opened the gates of heaven unto water torrential,
> and made the earth to gush with fountains,

and the waters met for a matter decreed.
And We bore him upon a well-planked vessel well-caulked
running before Our eyes—a recompense for him denied.
And we left it for a sign.
Is there any that will remember?
How then were My chastisement and My warnings?
Now We have made the Koran easy for Remembrance.
Is there any that will remember?

—The Moon. 54:8–17

The sura then continues with a similar story of an Arabian tribe, the people of 'Ād, who likewise were sent a messenger but did not listen to his warnings:

Ad cried lies.
How then were My chastisement and My warnings?
We loosed against them a wind
clamorous in a day of ill fortune continuous,
plucking up men as if they were stumps of uprooted palm
trees.
How then were My chastisement and My warnings?
Now We have made the Koran easy for Remembrance.
Is there any that will remember?

—The Moon. 54:18–22

Eventually, Muḥammad made clear to the Meccans that his intent was to reform their religious system, with Allāh as the only God worthy of worship. Not surprisingly, the Meccans turned against him, boycotting his clan and torturing slaves who became followers. This turning point is recorded by al-Ṭabarī in his account of the Satanic Verses (from which Salman Rushdie took the title of his famous book). It seems that the devil whispered false verses to the Prophet, causing him to preach a doctrine including the worship of the three most important

Meccan goddesses: al-Lāt, al-'Uzza, and al-Manāt, along with Allāh. That verse of the Qur'ān now reads: "Have you thought upon al-Lāt al-'Uzza and Manāt, the third, the other? Are yours the males and his the females? That indeed were an unfair division! They are but names which you have named, you and your fathers." (The Star. 53:19–20) According to al-Ṭabarī, though, Muḥammad made a mistake the first time around.

When the Messenger of God saw how his tribe turned their backs on him and was grieved to see them shunning the message he had brought to them from God, he longed in his soul that something would come to him from God which would reconcile him with his tribe. With his love for his tribe and his eagerness for their welfare it would have delighted him if some of the difficulties which they made for him could have been smoothed out, and he debated with himself and fervently desired such an outcome. Then God revealed: "By the Star when it sets, your comrade does not err, nor is he deceived, nor does he speak out of his own desire . . ." And when he came to the words: "Have you thought upon al-Lāt, al-'Uzza and Manāt, the third the other?" Satan cast on his tongue, because of his inner debates and what he desired to bring to his people, the words: "These are the high-flying cranes; verily their intercession is accepted with approval."

When Quraysh [Muhammad's tribe] heard this, they rejoiced and were happy and delighted at the way in which he spoke of their gods, and they listened to him, while the Muslims, having complete trust in their Prophet in respect of the messages which he brought from God, did not suspect him of error, illusion, or mistake.

—al-Ṭabarī, *History,* 108

Soon after, however, God revealed the correct verse to Muḥammad and he retracted his words of inclusion. The Quraysh tribe was incensed and began to actively persecute the Muslims. This event is thought to have occurred around the year 618. After this point, some of Muḥammad's early followers were forced to flee to nearby Abyssinia, while others remained with Muḥammad. After the death of his two most important supporters in 619, his wife Khadīja and his uncle Abū Ṭālib, Muḥammad himself became depressed and began searching for a new home. The suras of this period are no longer in the saj' of early exhortations, but are more proselike, with God at times comforting Muḥammad:

> We know indeed that it grieves thee the things they say; yet it is not thee they cry lies to, but the evildoers—it is the signs of God they deny. Messengers indeed were cried lies to before thee, yet they endured patiently that they were cried lies to, and were hurt, until Our help came unto them.
>
> No man can change the words of God; and there has already come to thee some tiding of the Envoys.
>
> And if their turning away is distressful for thee, why, if thou canst seek out a hole in the earth, or a ladder in heaven, to bring them some sign—but had God willed, He would have gathered them to the guidance; so be not thou one of the ignorant.
>
> —Cattle. 6:33–36

In this verse God appears to be speaking directly to Muḥammad, both reminding him of God's ability to send help in time of need and chiding him not to forget that God has all things under his command. From these examples, something of the intimate, almost conversational style of the Qur'ān can be seen. The Qur'ān is not so much a record of God's action in history, as it is a diary of God's revelation to his Prophet over time.

The culmination of Muḥammad's absolute dependence on God is found in the *Hijra*, the flight from Mecca to Medina, in the year 622. This year marks the new beginning for the community of Muslims and hence year one of the Muslim calendar.

But one should not forget that this flight was an act of near desperation, with Muḥammad and his followers leaving behind their families and tribes, who were their very source of identity. It is in Medina, in fact, that the word *Muslim* is first used, as Muḥammad's followers gain a new sense of identity in their *islām*, their submission to God.

With the growth of this religious movement, and its establishment in a new town, Muḥammad's role gradually moved from warner and exhorter to leader of the community. While he had probably always arbitrated disputes among the believers, his decisions were now being remembered and recorded. Muḥammad regulated the settlement of his followers in Medina and secured the position of the Muslims against their Meccan enemies through skirmishes involving several dozen men and women. The tradition remembers these events as "battles" and examples of God's intervention for the community. Eventually, the Muslim fighters were able to force the capitulation of Mecca to the Muslims in the year 630. By this time, the Prophet's authority had reached the point where any action he took was bound to be seen as precedent-setting by his followers. For instance, in the taking of Mecca, only four Meccans were killed resisting the Muslim forces. Nevertheless, these deaths broke the sanctity of Mecca as a town in which no killing was allowed. Muḥammad b. Isḥāq (d. 767) records the story of certain Muslims of the Khuzāʿa clan, who understood that the Prophet had set a new precedent, and took it upon themselves to kill an unbeliever of the tribe of Hudhayl.

Abū Shurayḥ said: When we were with the apostle the day after the conquest of Mecca, Khuzāʿa attacked a man of Hudhayl and killed him, he being a polytheist. The apostle arose and addressed us, saying, "God made Mecca holy the day He created heaven and earth, and it is the holy of holies until the resurrection day. It is not lawful for anyone who believes in God and the last day to shed blood therein, nor to cut down trees therein. It was not lawful to anyone before me and it will not be lawful to anyone after me. Indeed, it is not lawful for me except at this time because of God's anger against its people. Now it has regained its former holiness. Let those here now tell those that are not here. If anyone should say, The apostle killed men in Mecca, say God permitted His apostle to do so but He does not permit you. Refrain from killing, you men of Khuzā'a, for there has been too much killing."

—Ibn Isḥāq, *Life of Muhammad,* 555[6]

Here the Prophet is portrayed as being aware both of the power of his precedent and the possibility that his actions may be misinterpreted by later generations. This concern with rules and regulations of the community coincides with a shift in Qur'ānic revelation. While general rules about the importance of prayer and alms-giving had been revealed in the Meccan period, such as this brief verse: "The servants of the All-merciful are those who . . . call not upon another god with God, nor slay the soul God has forbidden except by right, neither fornicate" (Salvation. 25:64–67). Lists of rules in the Medinan period become much more specific. The following verse is usually dated to the earliest revelation in Medina.

O believers, prescribed for you is the Fast, even as it was prescribed for those that were before you—haply you will be godfearing— for days numbered; and if any of you be sick, or if he be on a journey, then a number of other days; and for those who are able to fast, a redemption by feeding a poor man. Yet better it is for him who volunteers good, and that you should fast is better for you, if you but know; the month of Ramadan, wherein the Koran was sent down to be a guidance to the people, and as clear signs of the Guidance and the Salvation. So let those of you, who are present at the month, fast it; and if any of you be sick, or if he be on a journey, then a number of other days; God desires ease for you, and desires not hardship for you; and that you fulfil the number, and magnify God that He has guided you, and haply you will be thankful.

—The Cow. 2:179–181

The Medinan suras also repeat the earlier exhortations and stories of past prophets, but rules on ritual, marriage, inheritance, and even slavery take on an increasingly important role. The unification of these themes is best seen in the Qur'ān's discussion of the pilgrimage to Mecca. The old Arabian rites of pilgrimage had included a procession around the Ka'ba (also known as the "ancient house"), but now these rites are recast by the Qur'ān as a monotheist tradition, originally established by Abraham, and later corrupted by the Meccans.

And when We settled for Abraham the place of the House: "Thou shall not associate with Me anything, and do thou purify My House for those that shall go about it and those that stand, for those that bow and prostrate themselves;

and proclaim among men the Pilgrimage, and they shall come unto thee on foot and upon every lean beast, they shall come from every deep ravine that they may witness things profitable to them and mention God's Name on days well-known over such beasts of the flocks as He has provided them: 'So eat thereof, and feed the wretched poor.' Let them then finish with their self-neglect and let them fulfil their vows, and go about the Ancient House."

—The Pilgrimage. 22:27–30

Even in these late suras, the Qur'ān never abandons its role as a teaching tool. It warns, exhorts, cajoles, and explains the true religion to the believers. While the Qur'ān occasionally addresses Muḥammad directly, it usually speaks to the believers, providing them guidance, and urging them to remember God's goodness.

It is remarkable that a tradition in which the Prophet is the sole source of revelation and yet also the leader of the community could maintain a clear distinction between divine word (God's revelation spoken by Muḥammad) and prophetic word (Muḥammad's uninspired advice and rules), and yet Islam preserves this distinction quite assiduously. This differentiation is all the more surprising given the fact that both Qur'ān and sunna were transmitted orally. There was, however, no attempt to make an authoritative collection of Muḥammad's words and deeds until over a century after his death, by which time all the early companions had died and individual stories had to be collected from the children, grandchildren, and students of these companions. As a result, there is not one, but several authoritative collections of hadīth. Very rarely, one of these hadith will contain a statement by God that is not found in the Qur'ān, but these are usually mystical and pietistic statements that have no legal authority in the tradition.

The process of gathering these individual stories explains the characteristic form of hadith, beginning with an *isnād*, a chain of transmitters, followed by the *matn*, the text of the story. For example, al-Shāfiʿī records this hadith:

> Mālik b. Anas told us from Ibn Shihāb al-Zuhrī from Anas b. Mālik, who said: The Prophet, riding on horseback, was thrown and his right side was scratched. Thereupon he performed one of his daily prayers sitting and we performed ours behind him sitting, too. After the prayer the Prophet said: "The prayer leader is expected to be followed; if he performs the prayer standing, you should stand, too; if he bows you should bow; if he raises his hands, you should raise them."
>
> —al-Shāfiʿī, *Risāla*, 200

In this case, the chain of transmission goes from al-Shāfiʿī to his teacher Mālik b. Anas. Mālik gets the hadith from his teacher,

Ibn Shihāb al-Zuhrī (d. 742 in Medina), a great collector of hadith and respected authority on law. Finally, al-Zuhrī takes the
story directly from Anas b. Mālik (d. 710), the companion of
the Prophet who was with Muḥammad on this occasion. Since
all of these figures are known for their trustworthiness in transmitting hadith, the hadith is considered to be authoritative.
The form of isnād and matn was also used for other authoritative statements, such as the earlier example from Mālik's
Muwaṭṭa', where he quotes a statement by 'Uthmān b. 'Affān,
the very caliph who collected the Qur'ān in 650. Mālik wrote:

> Mālik reported to us on the authority of his uncle Abū Suhayl b.
> Mālik, whose father heard 'Uthmān b. 'Affān while he was preach-
> ing and saying: Do not demand a wage from the female slave who
> has no particular skill, for surely when you demand this of her, she
> will earn her wage through prostitution.

These hadith are used to derive rules from the actions and
words of the Prophet's companions, but as mentioned by al-
Ghazzālī above, they are also considered to be authoritative by
Islam, and most hadith collections include both Prophetic and
companion hadith. For instance, Mālik's *Muwaṭṭa'*, although
not primarily a collection of hadith, contains 822 hadith from
the Prophet, 613 from his companions, and 285 from authoritative figures like his teacher al-Zuhrī, who never knew the Prophet.
Of the dozens of hadith collections compiled in the eighth,
ninth, and tenth centuries, two of the earliest (and shortest)
have been recognized as the most authoritative, those by
Muḥammad al-Bukhārī (d. 870 near Samarkand) and Muslim
b. al-Ḥajjāj (d. 875 in Nishapur?). These books (both entitled
al-Jāmi' al-ṣaḥīḥ, or *The Sound Collection*) are organized by subject matter, allowing the reader to find the Prophet's opinion on
every matter of religious importance. The fact that these ha-

diths exist in multiple collections and that individual hadiths can contradict one another, leads us back to the fact that these collections of hadith, however much they are revered by Muslims, are not sacred texts. Rather, it is the sunna of the Prophet that is authoritative for the tradition, while hadith is merely the form in which that sacred text is cast.

LITURGICAL, INTELLECTUAL, POLITICAL, AND RITUAL USES OF SACRED TEXTS

The primacy of the Qur'ān over the sunna as a sacred text can be seen in the fact that sunna is never utilized in a ritual fashion. According to al-Ghazzālī, chanting even a single letter of the Qur'ān is equivalent to ten good deeds to be added to all one's deeds at the end of time. Chanting 100 verses of the Qur'ān in the morning is like all the good deeds of the world. Yet, there is no such reward for reciting the sunna of the Prophet, other than the general reward bestowed on those who study and teach the religious texts of Islam. As a basis for Islamic law, one far richer than the Qur'ān, sunna is fundamental for determining the form and content of religious ritual, but once the ritual is established, the Qur'ān plays the central role.

The reason for the Qur'ān's centrality reaches back to the earliest period of the Islamic community, when the first Muslims came together for prayer. Early suras refer to recitations of the Qur'ān by the community, urging them to chant it "distinctly" or "in the night."

Thy Lord knows that thou keepest vigil nearly two-thirds of the night, or a half of it, or a third of it, and a party of those with thee; and God determines the night and the day. He knows that you will not number it, and He has turned towards you. Therefore recite of the Koran so much as is feasible.

—Enwrapped. 73:19

This chanting of the Qur'ān at night, also mentioned in the earliest historical accounts, is still performed by Muslims today. In the early period, however, the orality of the Qur'ān had another function. Among the Arabs, words could cut as surely as swords, particularly poems, which were thought to be inspired by spirits made of fire called *jinn*. Accounts are preserved of deadly serious encounters between feuding parties, where instead of fighting to the death each party casts versified aspersions on the other, competing in wordplay and rhyme, knowing that a clever phrase would be remembered and repeated for generations. The power of oral performance is also seen in this account of an early Muslim, 'Abdallāh b. Mas'ūd, who defiantly chanted the Qur'ān at the Maqām, the place next to the Ka'ba where Abraham, the father of the Arabs, also stood.

> In the morning he went to the sanctuary while Quraysh were in their conferences, and when he arrived at the Maqām, he recited, "In the name of God, the compassionate, the merciful," raising his voice as he did so, "the compassionate who taught the Qur'ān." (55:1) Then he turned towards them as he recited, so that they noticed him, and they said, "What on earth is this son of a slavewoman saying?" And when they realized that he was reciting some of what Muḥammad prayed, they got up and began to hit him in the face; but he continued to recite as far as God willed that he should recite. Then he went to his companions with the marks of their blows on his face.
>
> —Ibn Isḥāq, *Life of Muhammad*, 141–42

The harsh reaction of members of the polytheistic Quraysh tribe is evidence of the power oral recitation was understood to have. While Muḥammad made it clear that his revelations were not poems, he openly claimed that they were the words of God conveyed by the angel Gabriel. Accounts are also preserved of the recitation of the Qur'ān causing people to convert because of its matchless beauty, and Muḥammad called it his only miracle.

Once suras were revealed, they appear to have been memorized by the Muslim community, piece by piece. According to the traditional account, the first collection of the Qur'ān was made a few years after the death of the Prophet. It seems that in the early wars of conquest, the caliphs were concerned that many *ḥamalāti l-Qur'ān* (literally, "the carriers of the Recitation"), had been lost in battle. There is even a story that reports that 'Umar b. al-Khaṭṭāb (the second caliph, died 644) once asked about the meaning of a verse of the Qur'ān which he knew, but no one else did. Disturbed at these events, 'Umar began to collect the Qur'ān from various sources: both scraps of written suras and Muslims who had memorized certain suras. Even so, the earliest written Qur'āns were nothing more than mnemonic devices, written in an early Arabic script that did not differentiate between certain letters (*b, t, n, th,* and *y,* for instance, all of which were written in the same way), and that had no signs for vowels. So even with the writing down of the Qur'ān, the oral transmission of this sacred text remained primary among Muslims.

Once vowels and consonant markings began to be standardized for Arabic script, there was still a reluctance to use them for the Qur'ān. While this reluctance could be seen as an example of conservatism in a religious tradition, it is also an example of the primacy of a complex oral tradition, which valued memorization of the Qur'ān. Al-Ghazzālī records the following story about the gradual acceptance of such marks in the written text:

Al-Awzāʻī said, on the authority of Yaḥyā Ibn Abī Kathīr, "The Qur'ān was kept free of dots and vowel marks in its original form. The first thing that was introduced was the dotting of the letters *b* and *t,* maintaining that there was no fault in this, since it illuminates the Qur'ān. After this, large marks were introduced at the ends of verses, maintaining that there was no fault in this, since it marks the beginning of a verse. After this, signs were introduced, marking the ends and beginnings of Suras."

—al-Ghazzālī, *Iḥyā,* 1: 326

In fact, lack of such markings allowed for numerous variant readings of the text. These variants were compiled in the tenth century, with seven versions of the Qur'ān declared canonical, while seven others were declared noncanonical.

Today, the sacred quality of the Qur'ān in written form is demonstrated by the fact that it is the only book that is always printed in a fully vocalized fashion. That is to say, Arabic, like Hebrew, does not need vowels to be read, and most Arabic books and newspapers are written without them. The Qur'ān, however, is always written with all vowels, so that no one may accidently pronounce God's speech incorrectly. The tradition of variant readings lives on, however, in the fact that the very best Qur'ān reciters are able to chant the entire Qur'ān, from memory, in all seven ways. So while it has become standard to write the Qur'ān in only one way, oral recitation maintains the traditional variations.

For many centuries, elementary education in Islamic countries consisted exclusively of study of the Qur'ān. In these schools (known as *kuttābs*), children would learn to read and write Arabic, and to memorize the Qur'ān, a process that takes about three years. While colonization by European powers led to the dissolution of these traditional schools, memorization of the Qur'ān is still expected of any scholar or prayer leader (*imām*) in a mosque. For the daily prayers, all Muslims must memorize at least one sura of the Qur'ān, and many memorize more.

The importance of this essential orality of scripture in Islam cannot be overemphasized. From Gabriel's first command to Muḥammad ("Recite!"), to God's command in the Qur'ān to "chant the Qur'ān distinctly," to Muslims' concern to recite at least one sura of the Qur'ān in their daily prayer—whether they understand the Arabic or not, all this points to a conception of text that goes beyond Christian or Jewish experience of the Bible, or even Hindu experience of the Vedas. For the Muslim, recitation of the Qur'ān is an instantiation of the same revelatory event experienced by Muḥammad centuries ago. A. J. Arberry, the scholar of the Qur'ān whose translations are used here, explained his experience of the recited Qur'ān in this way:

> It is to the rhythm that I constantly return as I grope for a clue to the arresting, the hypnotic power of the Muslim scriptures. I was talking about this power to an Arab friend; before I could say what I would have said he spoke in terms that expressed exactly what was in my mind. "Whenever I hear the Koran chanted, it is as though I am listening to music; underneath the flowing melody there is sounding all the time the insistent beat of a drum." Then he added, "It is like the beating of my heart."[7]

Arberry also mentions that his first experience hearing the Qur'ān recited was during the holy month of Ramadan in Egypt. Ramadan is the month when the Qur'ān was first revealed to the Prophet, and to commemorate this event, Muslims fast during the entire day, consuming neither food nor water—not even cigarettes—until nightfall. In Islamic countries, life's rhythms adjust to this rigor, and people rest during the day and feast during the night. It is also common to recite the Qur'ān, or listen to recitation, during this month, and the Qur'ān has been separated into thirty sections for just this purpose. During her sojourn in Iraq in the 1950s, the ethnographer Elizabeth Fernea observed one Ramadan evening in the small Shī'ite village of El Nahra. In this village, women gathered every evening during Ramadan for *krayas*, ceremonies of prayer and pious meditation.

The Krayas in El Nahra were not often followed by Koranic readings, simply because most of the women could not read. Only at Laila's house, where the two middle girls, Laila and Basima, were in the sixth class of the girls' primary school, did this take place. . . . Laila was competent, but Basima was better than either. More intelligent than Laila and better educated than her mother, Basima seemed to sense the power of the words she was reading. They were not just groups of characters to her, and as she sat on the mat and read sura after sura in a slow, expressive voice, women would shake their heads, murmur to themselves, or raise their open hands to heaven in the traditional gestures of supplication. When she had finished, there would be a pause, a sort of hush before the women sighed, gathered their abayahs around them, and prepared to leave.[8]

It is worth noting that this recitation is not performed by a professional reciter or clergyperson, but by a young girl who happens to be adept at reading. In fact, the Muslim concept of authority is so firmly embedded in the sacred text, that the prayer leaders play a relatively minor role in devotional acts, and all Muslims are encouraged to experience the oral Qur'ān for themselves.

On a more mundane level, Prophetic sunna and Qur'ān play an active role in the daily lives of Muslims. Pious Muslims will undertake no commitment without saying *in shā' allāh* ("if God so wills)," as the Qur'ān instructs, and in response to a simple "how are you?" they may answer with the first words of the Qur'ān: "Praise be to God." Qur'ānic words are used as talismans to ward off evil and are found painted over doorways and on bumper stickers. A common piece of jewelry is a pendant with verses of the Qur'ān inscribed on it.

As for Prophetic sunna, pious Muslim men may wear a beard in imitation of the Prophet, or avoid striped clothing or silk as he did. Prophetic hadith are often quoted in discussion or in exhorting fellow Muslims to good deeds, and women wear the veil in imitation of the Prophet's wives. While none of these acts are required by the religion, their practice is seen as commendable.

Sacred text and authority are, then, clearly connected in Islam, yet not in the way one might expect. With all authority resting with God, it is obvious that the Qur'ān should be considered the only sacred text of Islam, and indeed, its primacy can be seen in its central role in Islamic rituals of prayer and fasting in Ramadan. This concentration of authority in a book of exhortation and warning, however, has forced Muslim scholars to find other sources of authority. On the one hand, the Prophet's sunna has proven very useful in explaining rituals and pious actions. But on the other hand, the relevance and relationship of all these laws requires the training of scholars like al-Shāfi'ī and al-Ghazzālī. Such scholars today use their human reason to interpret the Qur'ān and sunna, providing the vital, authoritative link to the sacred texts of Islam.

CHAPTER 3

Buddhism

HOW DOES BUDDHISM MAKE ITS ENDURING STATEMENTS? WHAT EXACTLY DOES BUDDHISM MEAN BY A TEXT?

As is the case with the other major religions in world history, the fundamental statements concerning enduring principles of ethics, practice, and philosophy that have been made by each of the various Buddhist traditions of Asia can be located within a set corpus of works, whose status as being universally valid and applicable has been recognized by its members. When speaking of a group of sacred texts that have come to be preserved in written form, the term usually applied by Western scholars of religion to such a collection of authoritative scriptures is "canon." Like the monotheistic religions of Judaism, Christianity, and Islam, the great Asian traditions of Hinduism and Buddhism also have their canons. However, at the outset of our discussion of sacred texts and authority, it is critical to note that there are several ways in which the standards for what constitutes scriptural canonicity in these Asian traditions have been markedly different from those of their monotheistic counterparts on the world religious scene.

There are four points worth making in this regard. First, when looking at a Buddhist canon, one finds that it is not based on one single scripture of focal importance, which is understood to function in the same way as the Torah, Bible, and

Qur'ān, do for Judaism, Christianity, and Islam, respectively. By comparison with the great monotheisms, the Buddhist canons are significantly larger in size, and much less centralized in focus. For example, the canon of the Theravada (Theravāda) Buddhists, which is referred to as the "Three Baskets" (Tripitaka [Tripiṭaka]) and includes 30 texts totalling 53 volumes written in the Pali language, is the smallest of the major Buddhist canons. The Chinese Mahayana (Mahāyāna) canon, called the "Great Scripture Store" (*Ta-ts'ang-ching*), consists of 55 volumes with 2,184 texts. And the largest of them all, the Tibetan Vajrayana (Vajrayāna) canon, made up of two parts known as the "Translation of the Buddha-word" and "Translation of Commentaries" (Kangyur and Tangyur), is comprised of 322 volumes containing 4,280 texts! Although they are indeed smaller in size, the canons of Judaism, Christianity, and Islam, as the reader will learn from other chapters in this volume, also surely extend well beyond their primary core text in scope, to include many additional works that provide their respective communities with further authoritative prescriptions. Nevertheless, these additional works almost inevitably tend to refer back to their canon's primary core text and its concerns. Thus, their functional relation to the core text of their tradition is quite consistently a directly commentarial and supplementary one. By contrast, while they are, as we will see, subject to hierarchical schemes that give certain works precedence in importance over others, the scriptures that make up a given Buddhist canon lack such a common primary source of reference.

Typically a Buddhist canon at the primary level is divided into several groups, each of which occupies its own particular area of instructive expertise that will be covered by many texts of more or less equal authoritative status. For example, the early Buddhist community identified three main areas of central concern, which established a common way of structuring canons that has been generally accepted by later developing traditions throughout history. The three main areas of instructive expertise are known as the three "trainings" (*shikshā*): (1) ethics, or morality (*shīla*); (2) meditative concentration, or equipoise (*samādhi*); and (3) insight into or understanding of the true nature of reality (*prajñā*). These three trainings have been made to correspond respectively with the traditional pattern of dividing the many primary texts of a canon into three "baskets" or sections: (1) community and individual discipline (Vinaya); (2) expository discourses on the practical teachings (Sutras [Sūtras]); and (3) systematic scholastic philosophy (Abhidharma). Given a structure such as this, Buddhist canons are comprised of not one but many primary texts, whose functional relation to one another is largely complementary. Furthermore, in addition to this primary level of scriptures which, as we will soon see, gain their authority by being considered the word of the Buddha (*buddha-vacana*), a Buddhist canon also contains a large secondary level of texts, consisting of commentaries upon the primary texts, composed by later highly accomplished masters.

The second closely related point to be raised when speaking of the distinctive nature of Buddhist canonicity, is that the lack of a single, commonly followed core text also means that Buddhism, in its several distinct regional and sectarian forms, is not scripturally unified on a universal level, in a way similar to each of the three great monotheisms. The Judaic, Christian, and Islamic worlds have their own profound regional and sectarian differences as well, which account for significant canonical variations. But despite these divergences, the three religions have each remained united by their general agreement upon which scripture contains the divine revelation of ultimate truth. There is no such common consensus in Buddhism. As an example, let us point to a process of historical interpretation that will be investigated in greater depth later in this chapter. The primary discourses or sutras that Theravāda Buddhists have believed preserve the only authentic original teachings of Shakyamuni (Śākyamuni) Buddha (563–483 B.C.E.), were composed and compiled during the first five centuries of the religion, and they are held by Mahayana (Mahāyāna) Buddhists to be provisional, qualified versions of the truth (Dharma), publically taught by the Buddha to meet the lesser spiritual capacities of his first audiences. The primary scriptural dispensation that Mahayanists have maintained presents the Buddha's highest teachings, widely circulated among those of supposedly superior motivations in the early centuries of the common era, have in turn been superseded in the minds of the Vajrayana (Vajrayāna) Buddhists. Vajrayanists contend that the Mahayana sutras are true as far as they go, but they do not include certain esoteric teachings of the Buddha that are absolutely necessary for the attainment of complete enlightenment. These teachings, which are said to have been revealed only to practitioners of the highest level of spiritual preparation in works first appearing around the sixth century of the common era, go under the name of Tantras.

A brief third point, also closely related to the first two points, is that Buddhism differs from the major monotheisms in that it not only lacks a singular primary text around which a canon is centered and limited, but it has also never established any one core body of human authorities that has functioned in an equivalent manner to the rabbinate, episcopate, or caliphate, each of which has been charged with the determination of a single, fixed, closed list of sanctioned works for an entire tradition. This factor also contributes significantly to the greater size and diversity of the Buddhist canons.

The fourth and final way in which Buddhist notions of canon diverge from the standards privileged by the monotheistic religions has to do with criteria by which Buddhists have generally recognized texts as being "sacred," in the sense of being valid sources of religious truth of the most exalted value. In contrast to the holy books of Judaism, Christianity, and Islam, scriptures comprising a Buddhist canon are not deemed authoritative on the basis of being regarded as an exclusive revelation granted to humans by a supreme divine being. In principle, the ultimate significance of a given text for Buddhists lies less in the source from which it comes or in the literal meanings of its words, and more in its ability to generate the condition that their religion values most—awakening to the true nature of reality. Above all, texts are valued according to how efficacious they are in enabling persons to engage in ethical and meditative practices leading to an enlightened state of salvific insight and compassion, known as *bodhi,* which liberates them from suffering. Ultimately basing themselves on the hermeneutical standard of privileging the realization of bodhi or *nirvāṇa* (the "extinguishing" of the conditions of ignorance, passionate attachment, and aversion that lead to suffering) over source and word is another reason why Buddhist canons have tended to remain open to the inclusion of new sacred texts over the course of history. Later in this chapter, we will consider how sacred texts are used in Buddhism. We will not only acknowledge this most important function of scriptures, but will also examine how they can be utilized to serve other vital if less supreme purposes such as the accumulation of merit (*puṇya*) based on good actions (*karma*), an accomplishment that greatly protects and contributes to personal and communal welfare.

Having identified the noteworthy ways in which Buddhist ideas about sacred texts and their authority comparatively differ from the perhaps more familiar ones offered by the monotheistic religions, it would now be appropriate to bring into focus the question of how peculiarly Buddhist definitions of sacred texts have developed. Within Buddhism, any question concerned with determining authenticity, textual or otherwise, is perhaps best answered by first considering the tradition's general sources of religious authority, for it is upon recourse to these principal sources that all judgments about validity are finally made.

In Buddhism, it is maintained that the principal sources of authority are the "three jewels" (*tri-ratna*) in which all aspiring practitioners take refuge: Buddha, Dharma, and Sangha. "Buddha" refers first to Shakyamuni Buddha, the founder of the religion, whose historical and traditionally interpreted life story provides the ideal model for practitioners to follow. "Dharma," the second jewel, refers first to the Buddha's teachings, found in specific texts recognized as canonical by the particular tradition one joins.

Reginald Ray has made the important point that besides these key external and institutional conceptions of Buddha and Dharma, there are also within Buddhist traditions more internal and personal notions of where these sources of authority can be found.[1] With respect to the first jewel, *buddha* is also understood to refer to the ever abiding potential that all humans have to achieve the liberating realization of their own fundamental nature that was first attained in this world age by Shakyamuni Buddha's enlightenment (bodhi). Furthermore, it has been generally accepted that the attainment of enlightenment is not just an ever-present possibility, but is an actuality that many people throughout Buddhist history have accomplished. Given this assumption, Buddhists have been able to extrapolate and maintain that the "Dharma" jewel is discoverable not only in texts containing Shakyamuni's "teachings" ("Dharma" in the external, institutional sense), but also in the minds of all those who have realized "truth" ("Dharma" in the internal, personal sense) through their own ethical and meditative endeavors.

Once one grasps these connotations of Buddha and Dharma, the first two of the three traditional sources of authority, one is much better equipped to understand how Buddhists define their sacred texts. The sacred text par excellence is what Buddhists have called buddha-vacana, the "word of the Buddha." First and foremost, this means that anything containing discourses spoken by Shakyamuni is an authoritative sacred text, by virtue of its being buddha-vacana. Thus, the works Sutra and Vinaya taught by Shakyamuni Buddha are universally considered to be among the most sacred texts. However, since the authoritative jewels of Buddha and Dharma also extend to include all individuals who have attained the truth, the primateur of buddha-vacana can additionally be applied to any text that they compose, as they also teach from an enlightened perspective that does not depart from that of Shakyamuni. Thus, in addition to the Sutra and Vinaya of the Buddha, the various Buddhist canons are filled with a variety of compositions—commentaries, Abhidharma treatises, meditation manuals, sermons, autobiographies—attributed to their tradition's enlightened sages.

Beyond this, the wider interpretation of the concepts of Buddha and Dharma has led Buddhists, particularly Mahayanists and Vajrayanists, to speak of an even greater multiplicity of ways in which the true enlightened words can manifest themselves. For them, truth has not only been found in the texts containing the words of a Buddha named Shakyamuni who appeared to ordinary beings in a physical form known as the "physical body" (*nirmānakāya*); they further believe that it has also been found in teachings delivered to more advanced practitioners who could perceive the Buddha and other enlightened beings exhibiting themselves in a subtle, nonphysical divine form known as the "enjoyment body" (*sambhogakāya*). Finally, these Buddhists speak of a third kind of Buddha-body, known as the *dharmakāya* or "truth body." Basically, by asserting the existence of such a universally present "body," Buddhists are asserting that the whole of reality itself is a sacred text, in that the truth or Dharma as they define it, of a universe in which all phenomena exist only in conditioned, interconnected relation to one another, can be seen by anyone who develops the enlightened perspective of selflessness through meditation. Much of the Mahayana claim to possess a dispensation of sutras superior to that of the earlier schools—to whom the Mahayanists applied the pejorative collective label "Hinayana" (Hīnayāna, Lesser Vehicle)—is based on their belief that Buddha in enjoyment-body form gave more advanced teachings than in physical-body form. In a similar move, many Vajrayana lineages maintain their own claims to the highest teachings by tracing their lines of succession back to truth-body Buddhas.

The third source of authority, the jewel of the Sangha, can be defined as the community of Buddhists—lay and monastic—who follow the religion's specific life rules, maintain its teachings, and support and contribute to each other's spiritual development. The institution of the Sangha, by virtue of its preservation and approval of buddha-vacana and Dharma, has also played a crucial role in the determination of what becomes sacred text in Buddhism. The earliest Sangha was particularly important in this regard. First, many of its members' words are preserved in the Tripitaka, due to their being approved by or in accord with the Buddha. Second, many texts are judged to be authoritative because they are believed to come from elders in the early Sangha who received the Buddha's word and accurately passed it down. Thus, for a text to be considered an authentic Sutra, it must be introduced by a member of the Buddha's Sangha, who declares, "Thus it was heard by me at one time" (*evam mayā srutam ekasmin samāye*). Third, the first community should also be credited with establishing an important place for oral texts in Buddhism. At the First Council, convened by its leading members shortly following the Buddha's death, a tradition of monks functioning as *bhāṇakas* or "chanters" of buddha-vacana was begun, and it lasted in some early schools for well over 400 years, before conditions arose that forced the Sangha to decide that the texts would be better preserved if they were committed to writing.

The vital role that members of the Sangha, particularly those who are monks, have placed in the determination of textual authenticity is well evidenced. In the *Mahāpadesa-sutta* (*Discourse on the Great Authorities*), an early work that was well known and considered authoritative for later tradition, the Buddha pronounces the four "great authorities" (*mahapadesa*) from whom one may reliably receive a text as buddha-vacana:

> In a certain case, a monk may say, "Venerable Ones, I have heard and learned this myself from the mouth of the Blessed One himself, and this is the Master's dharma, vinaya, and teaching."
>
> Again, a monk may say, "In a certain locale, there resides a community (sangha) where there are elders and leaders; from the mouth of this community I have heard and learned this myself, and this is thus the Master's dharma, vinaya, and teaching."
>
> Again a monk may say, "In a certain locale, there reside a number of learned elder monks, in possession of texts, knowing by heart the dharma, vinaya, and summaries; from the mouths of these elders I have heard and learned this, and this is thus the Master's dharma, vinaya, and teaching."
>
> Again a monk might say, "In a certain locale there lives a single elder monk, who is learned and who is in possession of texts, knowing by heart the dharma, vinaya, and summaries; from the mouth of this elder, I have heard and learned this, and this is thus the Master's dharma, vinaya, and teaching."

Clearly, one of the reasons why monks have enjoyed the highest status in Buddhist communities is the responsibility they have borne as guardians of texts and arbiters of truth-claims. In another early account, we find the point made that even when a monk has heard the very words of the Buddha, he is not to repeat them merely out of reverence, but may do so only on the condition that he has comprehended their meaning. After a particularly important discourse, the Buddha addressed the monks in these terms: "Will you say, 'honoring the Master and, through respect for the Master, we will say this or that?' 'We will not do so, Master.' 'What you affirm, is it not what you yourselves have recognized, seen, and grasped?' 'It is just so, Master'" This episode is indeed a telling one, for it appears to assert that the monks' own understanding must take precedence, even in the matter of the words of the Buddha himself. As we will continue to see in this chapter, the ultimate standard by which a text's authenticity and authoritativeness is judged is its ability to be effectively conducive to generating an understanding of the true nature of things (*dharmatā*), which alone brings about an enlightened salvation from suffering. Support for the position that ultimately a text must accord with the true nature of things is found throughout Buddhist literature, including the previously mentioned *Discourse on the Great Authorities,* which clearly goes on to say that the four great authorities alone are not enough to determine the validity of buddha-vacana:

> If a monk says this, "Venerable ones, in a certain kingdom, I heard and received this teaching," you must neither accept nor reject what he tells you. It is necessary, relying on sutra, to examine what is true and what is false; relying on vinaya, relying on the abhidharma, to examine what is essential and what is adventitious. If the teaching proposed is not sutra, not vinaya, not abhidharma, then you must say to him, "The Buddha has not said that, you have incorrectly learned it. Why? Because I have relied upon sutra, vinaya, and abhidharma, and what you have said is in contradiction with dharma."

Keeping in mind that the term *Dharma* connotes both the Buddha's teachings as found in scriptures and the true nature of reality, one might well ask what Buddhist truths this discourse is referring to when it instructs one to rely on Sutra, Vinaya, and Abhidharma texts. The *Nettippakarana*, a Theravada treatise on textual interpretation, provides an answer when it states:

> With what sutras is it necessary to compare the texts? With the four noble truths. With what vinaya should one compare them? With the restraint of the three poisons of passion, hatred, and ignorance. Against which abhidharma should one measure them? Against the doctrine of dependent origination.

The three truths mentioned here—the Four Noble Truths, the three poisons, and dependent origination, are the core of Buddhist thought and practice. In brief, they teach us that while our failure to realize the impermanent, conditioned nature of all things lead us to acts of passionate attachment and aggression, which only cause suffering, the path of compassionate ethics, meditation, and wisdom can lead us to freedom from suffering.

For Buddhists, the concerns of establishing criteria to determine textual authority are closely associated with issues of scriptural interpretation. Once a text's authenticity has been confirmed and the work has been placed within a canon, the question of how it should be approached and understood arises. While it is not possible here to discuss the details of the whole Buddhist hermeneutical enterprise, it is useful to at least briefly note its major principles. The guidelines for the proper interpretation of authoritative texts are found in their definitive form in a formula known as the "four reliances" (*catuhpratisaraṇāni*):

> The dharma is the reliance, not the person.
> The meaning (artha) is the reliance, not the letter (vyañjanana).
> Those sutras whose meaning is definitive [(nītārtha) are the

refuge], not those whose meaning is interpretable (neyārtha).
Intuitive knowledge (jñāna) is the
refuge, not conceptual thought (vijñānam).

What is interesting for our purposes here is that this founda-
tional statement of Buddhist hermeneutics establishes a hierarchy of values that is entirely consistent with the tradition's
stances on textual authority. The first statement echoes the *Discourse on the Great Authorities* in finding teachings that reflect
the nature of things more reliably than human opinion. The
preferability of adhering to a text's substance rather than to its
style may be obvious, but we may understand Buddhism better
if we note that the term for "meaning," *artha,* has the connota-
tion of useful, goal-oriented meaning. Thus, sutras that are
definitive rather than subject to interpretation are preferred, because they more immediately and directly affect the practitioner. Finally, the establishment of intuitive knowledge as the
highest reliance reflects the Buddhist tendency to emphasize
personal realization as the ultimate source of understanding.

WHAT ARE THE PRINCIPAL
SACRED TEXTS OF BUDDHISM?
THE FORMS THEY TAKE

Given the nature of the Buddhist canons previously discussed
in this chapter—their continual open-endedness; their tremendous variety along regional, traditional, and sectarian lines;
their enormous size; their lack of a single, core text, etc.—one is
forced to conclude that it is practically impossible to answer the
above question. On the one hand, if one attempts to narrow the
field and select a few outstanding representative texts, one runs
the great risk of essentializing Buddhist traditions to a degree
that would appear unrecognizable to their practitioners. On the
other hand, if one endeavors to identify all of the texts that various major Buddhist groups consider principal, one would

likely end up presenting something not much more than a catalogue list.

Having said this, one must then quickly proceed to acknowledge that the above question has often been a vital one for Buddhists, especially for those living in cultures where Buddhist traditions have only recently been introduced. Faced with a large and bewildering array of texts, whose teachings appear upon comparison to be wildly divergent despite their common claim to be the word of the Buddha himself, Buddhists in various cultures over the course of history have been forced to develop strategies for answering this very question of what are the religion's most important texts. Here, it might well prove instructive to investigate a particular historical example of a culture's attempts to solve this dilemma.

The subject of our case study will be China in the fifth to seventh centuries of the common era. The Mahayana form of Indian Buddhism that was being imported at this time, after a gradual period of introduction over the first four centuries of the millennium, was by no means a homogenous and consistent system, but was rather a very well-developed yet complexly diverse tradition. Increased translation activities, monastic enrollments, and popular patronage had further familiarized the Chinese with Buddhism, but they remained confused by their encounter with such a mass of often contradictory philosophies and practices. In response, they tried to rectify the differences they saw.

Scholars of Chinese Buddhism have identified three types of strategic solutions devised by Chinese Buddhists to come to terms with the unwieldy Mahayana canon. The first solution, which was largely unsuccessful, was to earnestly imitate certain Indian antecedents, by accepting the texts of just one Indian school and rejecting the others. The two major products of this response were the "Three Treatise" (San-Lun) and "Dharma Characteristics" (Fa-hsiang). Schools who tried to make sense of the many different Mahayana Sutras through the exclusive interpretive lenses of the Indian "Middle Way" (Madhyamika [Mādhyamika]) and "Mind Only" (Cittamatra [Cittamātra] or Yogacara [Yogācāra]) philosophical schools, respectively. Despite making significant advances in the Chinese understandings of important Indian Buddhist doctrines, these schools failed because their narrow, reductive approaches never caught on outside intellectual, elite circles. Two other examples of this first kind of solution, the Vinaya and Abhidharma schools, were obviously doomed to an even more rapid demise, considering that both were solely devoted to engaging only one of the three major collections of scripture.

The second type of attempted solution was a more viable if ultimately flawed one. Following the distinctively Chinese religious inclination to harmonize things, certain prominent Chinese Buddhist leaders tried to accept all of the Buddha's teachings, by implementing eclectic but hierarchical ordering systems. Based on the key Mahayana idea that enlightened beings use "skillful means" (*upāya*) to adjust their teachings to the varying capacities of their audiences, these thinkers maintained that while all buddha-vacana is at least partially or provisionally true, there is only one sutra that contains the ultimate, uncompromised truth. The most inclusive of this type of interpretive scheme was engineered by the T'ien-t'ai ("Heavenly Terrace") School and its eminent founder Chih-i. Chih-i sought to embrace all Buddhist teachings within a single doctrinal system, by categorizing them hierarchically according to different periods of the Buddha's life. Chih-i maintained that the Buddha gradually revealed higher and higher teachings over the course of his career, as his audiences presumably grew to understand him better and better. According to T'ien-t'ai, in the three-week period immediately following his enlightenment, the Buddha tried to deliver the very advanced *Flower Garland Sutra,* but no one was capable of comprehending it. Accordingly, he spent the next period of twelve years adjusting his teachings, beginning with basic ideas like the Four Noble Truths and Dependent Origination, which are the hallmarks of the Theravada and other so-called Hinayana (Lesser Vehicle) schools. The third phase took up eight years and is known as the "Time of Rebuke," for the Buddha rejected Hinayana teachings in a favor of the *bodhisattva* ideal of universal compassion and salvation. For the next twenty-two years the Buddha entered the "Time of Reconciliation," when he taught the essential unity of the Mahayana and Hinayana teachings that all phenomena are empty (*shūnya*) and without self (*anātman*), respectively. Finally, in the last eight years of his life, the Buddha taught the teaching that Chih-i considered ultimate, the *Lotus Sutra*. The T'ien-t'ai School and its counterpart in syncretism, the Hua-yen ("Flower Garland") School, were even more scholastically influential than their more exclusivist predecessors. But their philosophical inclusivism limited their memberships to the most motivated academic types, and their spiritual eclecticism led them to construct systems of meditation that were largely impractical.

Despite their failure to develop systems that could be widely practiced, the schools involved with the first two solutions for integrating the Mahayana canon paved the way for the success of the third type of Chinese response, which produced the two major forms of East Asian Buddhism, the Meditation (*Ch'an* in Chinese; *Zen* in Japanese) and Pure Land (*Ching-t'u* in Chinese; *Jōdō* in Japanese) schools. With philosophical sophistication already established, both schools were able to selectively simplify their doctrinal statements, and focus on the exclusive and intensive pursuit of one particular practice. Ch'an/Zen, with its rigorous application of self-disciplined contemplative techniques, and Pure Land, with its focus on faithful recitation of the name and total dependence on the saving grace of the celestial Buddha of Endless Light (*Amita* in Chinese; *Amida* in Japanese), became enormously successful traditions.

THE USES OF SACRED TEXTS

In this last section of the chapter, we will attempt to explore some of the ways in which Buddhists have practically applied their scriptures to meet a variety of human needs. Ultimately, the major religious traditions of the world have soteriological aims, and they use their sacred works didactically to achieve such goals. In other words, the great religions are concerned above all with liberating humanity from worldly suffering, and their texts—written, oral, and artistic—are most frequently utilized as guides that when read, heard, or observed, teach individuals how to best achieve such a state of spiritual salvation. This being said, it must also be granted that humans have been ardently engaged in other pursuits—such as building of community, securing and protecting of health and material welfare, and establishing social and political independence and strength—which have had an importance that arguably has often equaled if not surpassed the soteriological endeavor. Not infrequently, these more mundane endeavors have been seen by religious traditions as quite necessary supports, which can contribute more or less directly to the process of eventually attaining salvation.

With these considerations in mind, let us now survey some interesting examples of three important usages of sacred texts—liturgical, ritual, and political—that Buddhists have traditionally employed.

The Liturgical Use of Sacred Text:
The Public Recitation of Monastic Rules

When one considers, as we have done, the many differences Buddhists have had with respect to which texts expound the most superior philosophical doctrines, it becomes all the more astonishing to observe the remarkable extent to which they have traditionally agreed about moral principles, particularly with regard to those of Buddhist monks, who have always been looked to as vital sources of authority and objects of veneration within the Sangha. The whole of the monastic course of ethical discipline is contained in a scriptural collection known as the Vinaya. Because all of its more than 200 rulings concerning conduct within the monastery have always been considered to be ones that the Buddha himself decided upon as particular situations arose within the original community, the Vinaya has enjoyed the authority of being buddha-vacana. It was pronounced as such at the First Council, and ever since that very early point, the Vinaya has been followed to a degree of uniformity which the Sutra and Abhidharma texts have never commanded. While philosophical arguments about the meaning of commonly held sutras and the authenticity of competing dispensations of sutras have abounded in Buddhist history, and have surely brought about their own fair share of divisiveness, they have never been perceived to be as great a threat to the unity of the community as the much less frequent disputes over proper adherence to the Vinaya have been. Historically, an official schism (called *sangha-bheda,* or "community-break") has always been declared when a group of monks decides to modify the Vinaya, but never when doctrinal divergences arise. This is evidenced in Indian Buddhist history, when groups of monks who shared very similar versions of the *Sūtra-Piṭaka,* but differing versions of the *Vinaya-Piṭaka,*[2] were often forced to live apart, while Hinayanists and Mahayanists often lived together under a common monastic code, despite their fierce disagreements over doctrinal matters.

The Vinaya at its core has come to be expressed in a litany of disciplinary offenses known as the *Pratimoksha.* There are over 200 rules for monks and over 300 for nuns listed in the *Pratimoksha.* They range from major transgressions against the principles of nonviolence and sexual continence, which result in expulsion from the Sangha or probation, to more minor violations of interpersonal harmony and self-control, which can be righted by a simple act of atonement or confession. For the Sangha in the Theravada countries of Sri Lanka, Cambodia, Laos, Thailand, and Myanmar (Burma), the most frequently celebrated and important liturgical ceremony is the bimonthly occasion, set on "Uposatha" days at the end of every lunar fortnight, when monks gather together in a special meeting hall, usually following a period of fasting, to collectively chant this code of prohibitions known as the *Pratimoksha*. The recitation of this text serves many purposes, not the least of which is the reaffirmation of unity within the community of monks (*bhikshu-sangha*). At the very beginning of the text, the monks are indeed exhorted to move in this direction: "Members of the community who lived united, in friendship and without disputes, are happy. Recite together and live in comfort!" Above all, as a formal declaration of unfailing adherence to the rules of discipline, in which each monk has the opportunity to confess any transgressions, it is intended to restore and maintain the purity (*parisuddhi*) of the Sangha. All fully ordained monks within the bounds of a particular monastery are required to attend. The selection given below includes the ritual prelude to the ceremony, as well as the first four rules, which entail expulsion from the Sangha:

> May the community hear me, Venerable Ones! Today is the day of Uposatha, the fifteenth day of the fortnight. If the community is ready, let it perform the Uposatha ceremony and recite the Pratimoksha. What is the community to do first? It must recite the declaration of purity. I will recite the Pratimoksha. Let all of us here listen and pay attention. Whoever has committed an offense must declare it. Whoever is without fault must keep silent. From your silence, I will infer that you are pure. Just as a single man must answer a question addressed to him, so it is in this gathering, when a question has been repeated three times. A monk who does

not confess an offense which he has committed and which he re-members, once the question has been asked three times, is guilty of deliberate lying. And deliberate lying, Venerable Ones, has been declared by the Master to be an impediment to progress on the path. This is why a monk who has committed an offense, who remembers it and is intent upon purification, must declare his offense, Disclosing it will be beneficial to him.

O Venerable One, we will perform the Uposatha ceremony and recite the Pratimoksha.

These are the four cases involving expulsion:

1. A monk who has undertaken to live his life according to the moral precepts of monks and who has not renounced these precepts, or formally announced his inability to follow them, if he indulges in sexual intercourse with another human be-ing, or with an animal, he is expelled and no longer allowed to take part of the community.

2. A monk who stealthily takes something that was not given to him, in a village or a forest, such that it would merit his being arrested by a king, being executed, jailed, or exiled, and being told, "You are a thief, a fool, an aberrant, a sneak!"—he is ex-pelled and no longer allowed to be part of the community.

3. A monk who intentionally takes the life of another human being, who finds a weapon for someone else and extols the beauty of death, or who incites them to kill themselves by planting thoughts in their minds with words such as these: "O friend, of what use to you is this life of suffering and evil? You would be better off dead!"—such a monk is expelled and no longer allowed to be part of the community.

4. A monk who lets it be known that he has supernormal attain-ments, though he has none, or that he has knowledge and in-sight like those of enlightened persons, and who says, "I

know this, and see that,"—unless he was mistakenly overestimating his achievements—such a monk is expelled and no longer allowed to be part of the community, even if later on, . . . wishing to purify himself, he should admit that he was lying, engaging in vain and idle talk, claiming to know what he did not know, claiming to see what he did not see.

Venerable Ones, the four cases involving expulsion have been recited. Any monk who admits to any one of these can no longer reside with the monks. Venerable Ones, I ask you, "Are you completely pure on these points?" (The leader repeats this twice more). The Venerable Ones are completely pure on these points, and therefore they are silent. Of this, I am taking note.

Such a unified expression of an ideal serves to acknowledge, legitimate, and perpetuate the community of monks as the authentic bearer of the spiritual path articulated by the Buddha. It is also a cultic celebration of the principle of the Buddha's path—self-discipline—that enables individuals to overcome their passionate, aggressive, egocentric conditioning. As such, the Pratimoksha recitation provides an opportunity for monks to purify themselves individually while living communally. While chanting, the monks are expected to undergo a thorough self-examination. This is said to purify both the Sangha and its individual members completely, in body, speech, and mind. In terms of the body, the monks are physically gathered together as one. With regard to speech, they are chanting in unison. Mentally, the opportunity to confess their offenses leaves them with no doubts about their personal ethical behavior.

The Ritual Use of Sacred Text: The Mahayana "Cult of the Book"

As part of a popular religious movement with many devotional elements, the practices of Mahayana Buddhism, whether aimed at directly pursuing bodhi or securing more mundane rewards such as health, wealth, and power, have been largely carried out in religious environments that place great faith in the enormous assistance and support that people can receive from the tradition's pantheon of Buddhas and bodhisattvas, with their inexhaustible stores of merit and supernormal power. Of particular interest to us in this regard is the development of widespread reverence toward Mahayana sutras, such as the *Lotus Sutra* and those in its "Perfection of Wisdom" collection, as sources of the Buddha's presence and power. Since their appearance in the early centuries of the common era, Mahayana sutras have been seen not as just expressions of truth, but as embodiments of the Buddha's qualities of compassionate activity, wisdom, and power. A major concern of Mahayanists as well as Vajrayanists, whose main texts, known as tantras, arose about 500 years later, has been with establishing personal connections with Buddhas and bodhisattvas and their qualities. For them, texts that can be copied and recited are neither distinguishable from the Buddha, whose words they are, nor from enlightened qualities. Thus a person who is copying, reciting, or engaging in other forms of "text worship" (*sūtra pūjā*), such as making offerings to a text and its preachers and giving joyful attention to the Dharma it conveys, has direct access to the enlightened qualities.

As the cult of the book developed, there came about a particular proliferation in the usage of short verbal formulas found in the Mahayana sutras and Vajrayana tantras. Known as *mantras* or *dharanis* (*dhāranīs*), they were believed to magically bestow benefits upon those who recited them correctly. Understood as concentrated expressions of truth that embody the protective power of a Buddha or bodisattva, mantras and dharanis became popular because they were easily performable techniques for establishing connections with and receiving empowerments from Buddhist deities. At the same time, whole sutras also continued to offer powerful mundane and transmundane accomplishments. Perhaps the most famous text in this regard is the *Lotus Sutra*. The most popular and influential Buddhist text in East Asia, the *Lotus Sutra* has been important for a great number of reasons. Not the least of these is the immense amount of attention it has received as object of worship, no doubt due in large part to its relentless promotion of the many benefits it can provide, to those who revere it through a variety of ways such as offerings, copying, recitation, study, teaching, and meditation. The following passage is a typical example of the rewards available to those who use the *Lotus Sutra:*

> If one who has had the teachings passed to him, receives blessings that are immeasurable, how much more so one who in the Dharma assembly first hears this sūtra and responds with joy. Suppose someone encourages another person, urging him to go and listen to the Lotus, saying, "This sūtra is profound and wonderful, hard to encounter in a thousand, ten thousand eons!" And suppose, as urged, the person goes to listen, even though he listens for just a moment. The blessings that the first person gets in reward I (Buddha) will now describe in detail:
>
> Age after age, no afflictions of the mouth, no teeth missing, yellow or blackened, lips that are not thick, curled, or cleft, no hateful features, a tongue not dry, black, or too short; nose high, long and straight, forehead broad, smooth, and well-shaped, face and eyes all properly aligned and impressive, the kind people delight to look at, breath free of foul odor, a fragrance of utpala flowers constantly emitted from the mouth. Suppose one goes to the monks' quarters expressly to listen to the Lotus Sutra and listens with joy for just a moment—I will now describe the blessing. In existences to come among heavenly and human beings, he will acquire wonderful elephants, horses, carriages, palanquins adorned with rare jewels, and will mount to the palaces of heaven. If the Dharma is expounded, and one encourages someone to sit and hear the sutra, the blessings he acquires will enable him to gain the seat of a Shakra, Brahmā, and Universal Ruler. How much more

so if one listens single-mindedly, explains and expounds the meaning, and practices the sutra as the sutra instructs—that person's blessings know no bounds!

Not only did the *Lotus Sutra* itself promote the wide-ranging benefits available to those who used it, but in China a whole genre of indigenous narrative tales, called "Records of Miraculous Response," arose with the specific mission of spreading the cult of the book. These "miracle tales," as they were also known, illustrate yet another way in which ritual and devotional culture contributed to the construction of sacred scripture and its meaning in Buddhism. The extraordinary stories enjoyed great popularity in medieval China, but not for the reasons one might expect. Behind the marvels that they recount, there remain constant injunctions to faith and piety. To this day, miracle tales circulate primarily for reasons of spiritual edification, although their appeal can also be attributed to their very evident humor and entertainment value. The selection below, is taken from a Tang Dynasty (sixth to ninth centuries of the common era) collection entitled "Accounts in Dissemination and Praise of the Lotus Sutra," famous for its tellings of extraordinary devotion to the text:

> There was a certain nun, her name forgotten, who lived on the outskirts of Kunshan district of Suzhou. She became a nun at an early age and took to constant recitation of the *Lotus Sutra,* which she performed devotedly twice a day for some twenty-odd years. In appearance she was unusually beautiful and refined, so much so that anyone who caught sight of her was struck immediately with affection for her. During the first year of the Yongchang era (689) a certain district office manager named Zhu began to entertain wicked fantasies about her and sought to press her with his less than honorable designs. Yet the nun remained firm in her chastity and refused to give in to him.

Angered by her rejection, Zhu made a great deal of trouble for the abbey and intentionally sought to disrupt their regular means of livlihiood. The nuns were at a total loss as to where to turn to rid themselves of this plight. Whereupon, the nun who kept the *Lotus* said, "How could the *Lotus Sutra* fail to show its spiritual potency in this matter?" She then donned her purified robe, entered the Buddha hall, burned incense, and professed vows.

Not long thereafter the office manager, availing himself of some official pretext, came to the abbey to pass the night. His heart, of course, harbored other intentions. But the very instant he sought to find his way to the nun's quarters, his lower extremities were seized with a burning pain and his male member dropped off. Rivulets of perspiration streamed from his skin, leprous ulcers broke out over his body, and his eyebrows, beard, and sideburns all fell out. The office manager grievously recanted, but even after trying one hundred remedies, he still was never completely cured.

The Political Use of Sacred Text: A Japanese Case

In Japan, fervent faith in the potent workability of a religious transaction, in which a devotee's ritual use of a text is exchanged for the powerful intervention of a Buddha or bodhisattva, was frequently brought into the political realm. Again, the *Lotus Sutra* has played an enormous role. As far back as the Heian Period (ninth to twelfth centuries of the common era), leading monks from the Tendai School (the Japanese version of the aforementioned T'ien-t'ai School from China) used various rituals associated with the *Lotus* to purchase political power, and as recently as the late twentieth century, a popular "New Religion," the Nichiren Shoshu, whose members are known for their singular faith in the power of chanting the title of the *Lotus* (*"namu myoho renge kyo"*), has made significant political inroads on both the local urban and national scene, with the growing success of a branch party called the Soka Gakkai.

However, the use of Buddhist sutras as tools to guarantee the power and prosperity of the nation and its rulers has had an even longer history in Northeast Asia, with the seminal text being the *Sutra of the Sovereign Kings of the Golden Light.* The *Sutra of the Golden Light,* as it is known for short, contains a most thorough discussion of the responsibilities of the ruler and the relation between the state and Buddhism. This masterpiece of Buddhist literature played a more important role than any other scripture in establishing Buddhism as the religion of Japan in the Nara Period (eighth century), and its influence continued undiminished for centuries. The sutra opens with an eloquent Mahayana-style proclamation of the Buddha's omnipresence and boundless compassion. The core of the text, however, is more concerned with the human cultivation of wisdom (prajñā), which must, the text asserts, guide the lives of all people, from the lowliest subject to the king himself. While the *Sutra of the Golden Light* gained much popular appeal for its depictions of the Buddha as a great healer, the rulers were most drawn to its chapter on laws, in which it declared that government and religion must be united under the Dharma, with peace and prosperity as their common ends. Japanese rulers in the Nara period held this sutra in such esteem that they attempted to make it an instrument of state policy. In the passage quoted below, we find four Divine Kings declaring their support to the Buddha for his promise to bless the ruler who is faithful to the Dharma:

> Most Revered One! When, in some future time, this *Sūtra of Golden Light* is transmitted to every part of the kingdom—to its cities, towns, and villages, its mountains, forests, and fields—if the king of the land listens with his whole heart to these writings, praises them, and makes offerings on their behalf, and if moreover he supplies this sūtra to the four classes of believers, protects them and keeps all harm from them, we Deva Kings, in recognition of

his deeds, will protect that king and his people, give them peace and freedom from suffering, prolong their lives and fill them with glory. Most Revered One! If when the king sees the four classes of believers receive the sūtra, he respects and protects them as he would his own parents, we four kings will so protect him always that whatever he wishes will come about, and all sentient beings will respect him.

CONCLUSION

In reflecting upon the preceding discussion of the uses of sacred texts in Buddhism, it is important to keep two points in mind. First, what has been presented here is intended only as a sampling of a multitude of ways in which Buddhists have practically employed their scriptures. While the examples investigated here do not amount to an exhaustive survey, they are, I would suggest, fairly representative of types of textual employment which have been commonly found throughout the Buddhist world. Second, while the liturgical, ritual, and political functions of sacred texts have met significant needs held by Buddhists over time, and in doing so they have done much to sustain the religion's long-lived viability in many Asian cultures, it is crucial to understand that these functions are of an importance that is ultimately secondary to that which is the primary role of scripture in Buddhism, which is a didactic and soteriological one.

It has been clear since the tradition's beginnings, when the Buddha is held to have plainly stated on his deathbed that his Dharma would remain in the form of Sutra and Vinaya, and then the early disciples began going about the business of preserving and propagating these works, that Buddhism's sacred texts have mainly served as vehicles for explicating the ethical, meditational, and philosophical teachings that guide the practitioner along the path to freedom from *samsara* (*saṁsāra*), the world of suffering. It has been a practically universal stance of

Buddhism that understanding and applying the contents of its major works does much to engender the liberative wisdom (prajñā) that is the religion's highest goal. For example, in the most important manual of religious practice in the Theravada tradition, a work entitled the *Visuddhimagga* (*The Path of Purification*), the great fifth-century master Buddhaghosa takes up over 800 pages in explicating one key sutra passage:

> When a wise man, established well in ethics,
> Develops meditative concentration and wisdom,
> Then, as an ardent and sagacious monk,
> He succeeds in disentangling this tangle.

At the outset of his work, Buddhaghosa responds to this verse by stating his intentions in composing his treatise:

> My task is now to set out the true meaning,
> Divided into ethics and the rest,
> Of this same verse composed by the Great Sage.
> There are here in the Victorious One's community,
> Seekers gone forth from home to homelessness,
> Who although desiring purification,
> Have no knowledge of the sure straight way—
> Comprised of ethics and the other two,
> Very hard to find, that leads to purification—
> Who, although they strive, attain no purification here.
> Pure in expositions, relying on the teachings of dwellers in the
>   Great Monastery,
> Let all those who desire purification,
> Listen intently to my exposition.

More precisely, sacred texts like the *Visuddhimagga* are held to be centrally involved in the cultivation of the first two of three progressively higher types of wisdom. As the final line of

Buddhaghosa's introduction indicates, the first type of wisdom is that which arises from listening (*śrutamāyī-prajñā*). It is incurred by hearing words or letters (*namān*) expounded as they were by the Buddha, and then arriving at a faithful acceptance of them.

Wisdom that arises from reflection (*cintamāyī-prajñā*), which follows the preceding, is also directly dependent upon sacred words. Reminiscent of the second of the "four great reliances" discussed above, this kind of wisdom is typically defined as a personal and reasoned understanding of the meaning (*artha*) of the teachings, which is over and above merely placing confidence in the letter. This level of comprehension of sacred text (in either oral or written form) is like that of the early monks, referred to earlier in this chapter, who could declare with assurance that they spoke not just out of respect for the Buddha, but also out of their personally grasping the truth of their own accord. If one is to set oneself firmly on the path to nirvana, however, one must eventually leave such dialectical, text-based types of wisdom behind. The Abhidharma texts classify both the wisdoms arising from listening and reflection as worldly (*laukika*) in nature, and associate them with a level of consciousness (*vijñāna*) that, while improved, is still discursive and defiled (*sāsrava*), subject as it is to the cravings, hatreds, and delusions that cause suffering. The most influential systematic treatise on the path, the *Abhidharmakosha*, compares the first level of wisdom to a flotation device that is constantly grasped by a person who cannot yet swim, and the second level to that same helpful device, which can sometimes be disregarded by a poor swimmer.

The only kind of wisdom, however, that is trandescendent (*lokottara*) and undefiled (*anāsrava*) is that which arises from meditation (*bhāvanāmāyī-prajñā*). Reminiscent of the fourth and final hermeneutical standard discussed above, wisdom that arises from meditation is based on a direct knowledge (*jñāna*), rather than on discursive consciousness (*vijñāna*). The *Abhidharmakosha* completes its analogy here by likening this third type of wisdom to a strong swimmer who can cross a river without any supportive aid. It is mediation alone, with its techniques for developing tranquility and concentration, and cultivating mindful attention to the experiences and events of life, without the imposition of habitually ingrained preconceptions and prejudices, that can lead one beyond the devotional and intellectual levels of comprehension founded on the textual lifesavers, to a fully experiential, integrated awareness that liberates one from the painful bondage of attachment to the fleeting things of this world. This much is clearly indicated by Buddhaghosa in his closing instructions to his monumental *Visuddhimagga*:

> Now that the exposition as set forth,
> Is almost free from errors and flaws,
> After bringing together all the expositions
> Of all these meanings, classified according to ethics and so
>   forth,
> Stated in the commentarial system of the five groups of sūtras,
> For this reason let meditators pure in comprehension,
> Now properly cultivate this Path of Purification.

Ultimately in every Buddhist's training, there comes a time when the supports and means of the tradition must be left behind. According to a metaphor found in one of the earliest sutras that would come to profoundly influence the tradition, including clearly the *Abhidharmakosha*'s author, Vasubandhu, and his analogy of the swimmer, one who has crossed the river (a referent to samsara) to the further shore (a referent to nirvana) has no further use for the raft. The later Mahayana and Vajrayana traditions also abound in sayings and images of their great masters that express this same message. The First Patriarch of the Ch'an/Zen (Mediation) School, Bodhidharma, is well-known for declaring that his brand of practice was,

A special transmission outside the scriptures,
Not founded upon words and letters;
By pointing directly to mind,
It lets one see nature and attain Buddhahood.

In similar fashion, a very influential later successor of Bodhidharma, the Patriarch Hui-neng, a figure credited with introducing a profound redefinition of his school's conception of meditation, is famously depicted in Zen art as gleefully throwing scriptures in a fire. Within the Vajrayana, Milarepa, the most celebrated Tibetan yogi, who spent most of his life in retreat in the Himalayas near Mt. Everest, declares to a scholar in one of his songs: "Texts? I don't need texts. Phenomena are all the texts I need." This statement is based on the important Buddhist idea, found in texts such as the *Flower Garland Sutra,* that the entire universe is a vast Sutra scroll, in the sense that the liberative insight into the empty nature of existence is discoverable in every single particle of dust.

The fact remains, however, that Buddhist traditions have consistently maintained that such a liberative realization is best sought through the agency of its supportive methodologies, at the heart of which is the sacred text. Only when the words are revered, well-learned, and integrated, can one take the final step, knowing what one is relinquishing, and how it can (and must!) be relinquished. After all, it is said that Hui-neng had his first major breakthrough after he heard the previous Patriarch preach the *Diamond Sutra's* discourse on emptiness, and in the same song quoted above, Milarepa acknowledges that it was only after receiving oral instructions from his teacher, Marpa, that he was able to meditate in solitude.

CHAPTER 4

Hinduism

HOW DOES HINDUISM MAKE ITS ENDURING STATEMENTS? WHAT EXACTLY DOES HINDUISM MEAN BY A TEXT?

Comparing religions, like the comparison of anything else, involves noting the differences between the compared entities as well as the similarities. Before providing answers to the questions, How does Hinduism make its enduring statements? and, What does Hinduism mean by a text?, let us begin by noting two areas of difficulty—of difference, or perhaps even of uniqueness and therefore absolute incomparability—that might give us pause as we turn to the case of Hinduism.

The first of these concerns is the very possibility of talking about "Hinduism" as if it were one religion rather than many. The conglomeration of religious traditions collectively known by this label incorporates a bewildering variety of sacred texts in which "enduring statements" of many and diverse kinds are encoded and preserved. Hinduism is, in fact, so disparate in this and other respects that some modern scholars have questioned the legitimacy of artificially unifying the multitude of traditions by applying to them such an umbrella term. Thus, for some, we cannot really speak about *the* Hindu attitude toward sacred texts and authority, but at best only a variety of attitudes in a variety of Hinduisms concerning a variety of sacred texts.

The fact of diversity—historical, cultural, linguistic, doctrinal, and sectarian—is, of course, true of other world religions also designated by a unitary label (e.g., "Christianity," "Judaism," "Buddhism," and "Islam"). Hinduism may be an extreme example, but it is hardly unique in this regard. Furthermore, in the case of Hinduism, as in other religions, certain themes can be identified that provide the scholarly basis for identifying conceptual unity within actual diversity. One of these themes might very well be the particular way in which Hindu traditions understand and use scriptural authority to legitimate a variegated set of beliefs and practices.

Religions in general are comparable in the kinds of claims to authority they make for their sacred texts and the truth claims embodied in them. In all cases, the appeal of religions is to transcendental or superhuman sources. Religious discourse is characterized by the attempt to surmount purely human and culturally and historically conditioned origins in order to represent a religion's truth claims as *objective, universal,* and *eternal*—in other words, as absolutely authoritative. It could be argued that it is, in fact, the peculiar and radical nature of these claims to transcendent authority that makes those traditions we call "religions" distinctive from traditions of other sorts.

Hinduism can be understood as a unified and continuous religious tradition in terms of the particular *sources* and *strategies* used to establish, legitimate, and maintain its religious authority. As we shall see, the most common way Hindus of various sorts do this is to appeal to the authority of the Veda, the most ancient and most universally acknowledged of the sacred texts of Hinduism. Other strategies for establishing authority for sacred texts are also to be found—e.g., attributing authorship to God, claiming transcendental powers of intuition and inspiration for a human author of the text, or basing authoritative claims on mystical experience—but these strategies themselves are already to be found in the paradigmatic sacred text that is the Veda. In any case, Hinduism, like other religions, regards its sacred texts as having their origins above and beyond the merely human.

The first area of possible difficulty in this comparative exercise in the case of Hinduism centers on the question of whether or not one can speak about "Hinduism" in the singular. The second problem revolves around the concept of sacred "text." What Hinduism means by a "text" is, generally speaking, not what many other traditions mean by this term. For in Hinduism, the "text" is most often *heard* rather than *read*; it is sacred *sound* rather than sacred *writing* that characterizes Hindu "scriptures."

The Veda, to take the paradigmatic case, is usually thought to be unauthored (either by a god or humans), but rather exists eternally in the form of sound. Ancient sages are said to have heard the Veda (or part of it) and then recited it to others. The Veda is, and continues to be, memorized syllable by syllable and transmitted orally by means of an intricate method of recitation. While ancient India certainly had a writing system by the middle of the first millennium b.c.e., it was only in very recent times that the oral Veda was written down.

The oral and recitative character of the Veda is also true of other Hindu sacred texts. Indeed, recitation of sacred texts forms the core of Hindu ritual life. Orally recited verses or formulas (*mantras*) are employed in meditational practices and in various Hindu ceremonies, and post-Vedic Hindu texts like the *Bhagavad Gita* (*Bhavagad Gītā*), the Puranas (*Purāṇas*), and the hymns of devotion composed by various poet-saints, are also memorized and recited, chanted, or sung as a means of acquiring spiritual merit. The seventeenth-century text called *Ramacaritamanasa* (*Rāmacaritamānasa*), a Hindi retelling of the *Ramayana* (*Rāmāyāṇa*) epic by the poet Tulsīdās, is recited both as a religious exercise and as popular entertainment, as are other post-Vedic texts. Although all of the Hindu sacred works are now available in printed editions, scripture in Hinduism remains recited scripture; the sacred "text" is here the oral "word."

In other cultures where texts are preserved orally, there tends to be a great deal of room for improvisation, change, and innovation; the oral nature of the text allows individual reciters to put their own distinctive marks on its retelling. Not so in India. The emphasis on the sacrality of sound and the rigorous methods devised for memorization—syllable by syllable—have insured that Hindu texts are precisely preserved over the ages. Learned Brahmins, who traditionally have been charged with the memorization of the holy books, are "walking Vedas." When the nineteenth century Indologist F. Max Muller was preparing his six-volume edition of the *Rig Veda* (*Ṛg Veda*), it was these learned Brahmins, and not any manuscript tradition, that he primarily relied upon for his published text.

Inevitably, some of those who memorize huge portions or the entirety of lengthy texts do not know the meaning of what they have memorized—and with the emphasis on the sacrality of sound itself, the meaning of the sound may be thought to be of secondary importance. But the tradition itself regards those who know both the text and its meaning to be better than those who have merely memorized the syllables, and those who put into action what they have memorized and understand are higher still:

> Those who read the books are better than those who do not know them; those who remember them are better than those who read them; those who understand them are better than those who remember them; and those who put them into action are better than those who understand them.
>
> —Manusmṛti 12.103[1]

THE CANONICAL AUTHORITY OF THE VEDA

Each of the many traditions and sects that comprise Hinduism has produced its own (sometimes overlapping) corpus of sacred texts, with their own justifications for their ultimate authority. In almost every case, however, these sectarian works are said to be based, in one way or another, on what constitutes the closest thing Hinduism has to a canon—the Veda.

Veda means literally "knowledge," and is a collective term for the enormous body of Sanskrit texts generated in the period from 1200 B.C.E., or before, to the middle centuries of the first millennium B.C.E. in North India. Allegiance to the authority of the Veda is perhaps the only attribute for designating "orthodoxy" within Hinduism, as many of the theologians of the tradition themselves have concluded. It can be argued that those Indic traditions arising subsequent to the Vedic era that have embraced the authority of the Veda, no matter how nominal that embrace may be, are by this definition "orthodox"; and the members of those post-Vedic traditions, by virtue of their allegiance to the authority of the Veda, may be categorized as "Hindu."

The Veda, like other canons, was deemed authoritative retroactively by those later traditions that established and aligned themselves to the canon. It was designated as "revealed" or "heard" (*shruti* [*śrūti*]) as opposed to all other post-Vedic texts, which were categorized as merely "remembered" or "traditional" (*smriti* [*smṛti*]). Furthermore, the "revealed" Veda was regarded as "not of human origin" (*apauruṣeya*), as opposed to the "traditional" texts, whose human authorship is acknowledged. The canonical powers attributed to any canon— as authorless (or authored by God) and thus outside the realm of particular individual or social interests; as eternal, and therefore not subject to the contingencies of historicity; as universal, and therefore not particular to any one social, cultural, or sectarian group; and as unquestionable and not subject to dispute—all these canonical powers are equally brought to bear on later Hindu texts that represent themselves as "Vedic."

Unlike some other religious canons, however, the Veda also

represented itself (and was not only represented later) as authoritative. The self-referential and absolute truth and authority of the Hindu canon was thus posited from its Vedic inception and reaffirmed in its later reception. The Veda is declared, in the Veda itself, equal to *satya* or "truth," or to "speech," or "the word" (*vac* [*vāc*]) also in the sense of "truth." Alternatively, the Veda is equated with the universal principle that is the ground and end of all knowledge and being, the *brahman* (e.g., Śatapatha Brāhmaṇa 10.1.1.8; 10.2.4.6). The Veda, it is said in the Veda, is "endless" like great mountains, while human knowledge of it is likened to mere handfuls of dirt (Taittirīya Brāhmaṇa 3.10.11.3-5).

The Veda also represents itself as timeless, before and outside history. The Veda frequently wrote itself into its accounts of the creation of the world, as is illustrated by the famous cosmogonic myth known as the "Hymn of Man," in which the universe is depicted as the product of a primordial sacrifice and dismemberment of the Cosmic Man:

> The Man has a thousand heads, a thousand eyes, a thousand feet. He pervaded the earth on all sides and extended beyond it as far as ten fingers. It is the Man who is all this, whatever has been and whatever is to be. He is the ruler of immortality, when he grows beyond everything through food. Such is his greatness, and the Man is yet more than this. All creatures are a quarter of him; three quarters are what is immortal in heaven. . . . When the gods spread the sacrifice with the Man as the offering, spring was the clarified butter, summer the fuel, autumn the oblation. . . . From that sacrifice in which everything was offered, the melted fat was collected, and he made it into those beasts who live in the air, in the forest, and in villages. From that sacrifice in which everything was offered, the verses and chants were born, the meters were born from it, and from it the formulas were born.
>
> —Rig Veda 10.90.1–3, 6, 8–9[2]

The "verses" born from this creative act of cosmic sacrifice ("in which everything was offered") are the components of the *Rig Veda,* the "chants" are the elements of the *Sama Veda (Sāma Veda),* and the "formulas" are the constituents of the *Yajur Veda (Yajur Veda).* The three principal sacred texts collectively known as the Veda (a fourth, the *Atharva Veda,* was included in the canon somewhat later) are here depicted as issuing forth, together with other elements of the cosmos, at the very beginning of time.

In some Vedic texts it is even said that the universe in its totality was originally encapsulated in the Veda and was generated out of it. In the beginning, Prajāpati, the "Lord of Creatures," "looked round over all existing things, and saw all existing things" in the Veda.

> For in that (Veda) is the body of all meters, of all hymns of praise, of all vital airs, and of all the gods. This indeed exists for it is immortal, and what is immortal exists; and this (contains also) that which is mortal. Prajāpati thought to himself, "Truly all existing things are in the Veda."
>
> —Śatapatha Brāhmaṇa 10.4.2.21–22

The sum total of reality, everything that exists, both immortal and mortal, is encompassed within the primordial Veda and comes forth out of it. Elsewhere we read that the Veda has two forms, one manifest (i.e., the scripture revealed to humankind) and the other wholly unmanifest and transcendent (Taittirīya Brāhmaṇa 2.6.2.3). In a somewhat later text, the Veda is also regarded as both immanent and transcendent. Both types of Veda are generated out of the cosmic principle, or *brahman,* but the transcendent Veda remains "secret" (Manusmṛti, 11.265–266).

Such canonical claims to absolute truth and primordial or even procreative status, already established in the Veda itself, were subsequently accepted, reinforced, and reapplied throughout the history of Hinduism. Many philosophical and theological authorities in Hinduism have insisted upon acceptance of the authority of the Veda as the mark of orthodoxy. Śaṅkara (c. 800 C.E.), the great teacher of the monistic philosophical school of Advaita Vedānta, determined heresy on the basis of whether any given doctrine or set of doctrines "contradicts the Veda." Kumārila (c. 700 C.E.), one of the principal authorities of the philosophical tradition called Mīmāṃsā, ranked all religions and philosophies on the basis of their stated adherence to the authority of the Veda. Buddhists, Jains, and others are heretical "for they do not accept the fact that the Vedas are the source (of their teachings), just as an evil son who hates his parents is ashamed to admit his descent from them."[3] Note here the notion that the teachings of these false religions are nevertheless said to spring forth from the Veda, which is, as we have seen above, equated with *all* knowledge, *all* truth. The main error Buddhists, Jains, and others make is to not recognize the Vedic source of their own religions!

In texts on religious and social law and duty governing all the classes of Hindu society, the Veda is similarly declared to be the all-encompassing source of true knowledge and the yardstick for measuring heresy. In the following passage from the Manusmṛti (c. 200 B.C.E.), the Veda's all-embracing virtues are extolled and those who deny its authority are reviled:

The Veda is the eternal eye of the ancestors, gods, and humans; the teachings of the Veda are impossible to master and impossible to measure; this is an established fact. All those revealed canons and various evil doctrines that are outside the Veda bear no fruit after death, for they are all traditionally known to be based upon darkness. The (teachings), differing from that (Veda), that spring up and die out bear no fruit and are false, because they are of a modern date. The four classes, the three worlds, the four stages of life, the past, the present, and the future, are all individually explained by the Veda. Sound, touch, form, taste, and smell as the fifth are brought to birth from the Veda alone; they are born in keeping with their qualities and their innate activities. The eternal teachings of the Veda sustain all living beings; therefore I regard it as the ultimate means of this living creature's fulfillment. The man who knows the teachings of the Veda is worthy of being general of the army, king, dispenser of punishment, and overlord of all the world. Just as a fire that has gained strength burns up even wet trees, so a man who knows the Veda burns up the fault born of his own action. A man who knows the true meaning of the teachings of the Veda becomes fit for union with ultimate reality even while he remains here in this world, no matter what stage of life he is in.

—Manusmṛti 12.94–102

Here again it is the Veda that is the primordial basis for "all living beings" and the fount of all knowledge and duty. Knowledge of the Veda makes one fit not only for rulership in this world but also for salvation, "for union with ultimate reality."

THE VEDIC AUTHORITY OF
LATER HINDU SACRED TEXTS

The first and most important source for the authority of the sacred texts of Hindus is thus Vedic revelation. A problem immediately arises, however. As we have seen above, it is only the Veda itself that is classified as "heard" or "revealed" literature of nonhuman origin; all other sacred texts of the various Hindu traditions are given lesser authority by being termed "remembered" or "traditional."

A second problem seems even more insurmountable. The great paradox of Hinduism is that although Hindu traditions are usually inextricably tied to the authority of the revealed Vedic canon, in later times the actual subject matter of the Veda was and is largely unknown and almost always irrelevant to the actual beliefs and practices proscribed in post-Vedic "remembered" or "traditional" sacred texts. The contents of the Veda (almost entirely concerning the meaning and performance of sacrificial rituals the vast majority of Hindus do not perform) are at best reworked (into ritual formulas or mantras for use in Hindu ceremonies), and often simply ignored.

How do post-Vedic sacred texts, in which the actual beliefs and practices of the various Hindu traditions are encoded but which are also technically classified as only "remembered," claim their authority? And if the contents of the Veda are by and large irrelevant to these post-Vedic Hindu texts, in what possible sense can Hinduism be said to depend on Vedic authority for its integrity as a religion?

One answer to this conundrum is that the Veda is not always treated as a closed canon. An example of the suppleness of the Veda is the fact that new sectarian Samhitas (Saṁhitās) and Up-anishads (Upaniṣads) (names for two genres of texts in the "revealed" Veda) have been composed throughout the history of Hinduism. New and non-Vedic teachings, doctrines, and prac-tices are packaged as "Veda," and in this purely nominal way "remembered" texts appropriate the authority of the "revealed" canon. The Veda, as Hindus use and supplement it, is thus something of an "open book."

Another strategy for lending Vedic authority to later "re-membered" or "traditional" texts is to blur or even erase the dis-tinction altogether. In the following quotation from the Manusmṛti, the Veda is acknowledged as the "root of religion" but "the tradition" and other sources of authority are also listed as equally authoritative and on a par with the canon:

> The root of religion is the entire Veda, and (then) the tradition and customs of those who know (the Veda), and the conduct of virtuous people, and what is satisfactory to oneself. Whatever duty Manu proclaimed for whatever person, all of that was de-clared in the Veda, for it contains all knowledge. So when a

learned man has looked thoroughly at all of this with the eye of knowledge, he should devote himself to his own duty in accordance with the authority of the revealed canon. For the human being who fulfills the duty declared in the revealed canon and in tradition wins renown here on earth and unsurpassable happiness after death. The Veda should be known as the revealed canon, and the teachings of religion as the tradition. These two are indisputable in all matters, for religion arose out of the two of them. Any twice-born man who disregards these two roots (of religion) because he relies on the teachings of logic should be excommunicated by virtuous people as an atheist and reviler of the Veda. The Veda, tradition, the conduct of good people, and what is pleasing to oneself—they say that this is the four-fold mark of religion, right before one's eyes.

—Manusmṛti, 2.6–12

"Revelation" and "tradition" are here wholly conflated, and to them are added two other sources for authoritative knowledge about religion: the customary practices of those who know the Veda (i.e., the Brahmins), the conduct of the "virtuous" or "good people" (i.e., also the Brahmins learned in the Veda), as well as personal conscience (what is "satisfactory" or "pleasing" to oneself). The last criterion in particular would seem to open up the possibilities for all sorts of non-Vedic belief and practice.

Other strategies have also been used to extend the authority of the Veda to Hindu texts. A very common one is to declare the post-Vedic sacred text to be the "fifth Veda." Both of the great Hindu epics, the *Mahabharata* (*Mahābhārata*) and the *Ramayana* (*Rāmāyaṇa*)—as well as many of the sectarian scriptures known as the Puranas (*Purāṇas*), which were composed in the first and early second millennia of the common era—have done just this to claim "Vedic" status. In other cases, sectarian works represent themselves as the quintessence of the Veda, or as simplified forms of the canon, or even as based on a "lost Veda" that is only now recovered (in the form of a Hindu text).

Similarly, the compositions of the great poet-saints of South India, who spearheaded the movement of ecstatic devotionalism directed to the deity Vishnu (Viṣṇu) or Shiva (Śiva), are widely known as "Dravidian Vedas." The poems of love and devotion composed by Nammalvar (Nammālvār) (ninth century of the common era) in particular are said to recount, in the Tamil language, the essences of the four Sanskrit Vedas and are regarded as fully equal in authority to the original Vedas. Indeed, all the works of the poet-saints of the South Indian sect known as the Śrīvaiṣṇavas are claimed to be clarified forms of the Veda composed in the language used by ordinary people of the region:

> We clearly understand the unclear Vedas from the songs of joy woven like beautiful Tamil garlands by Poykai (and all the other alvars [poet-saints]). Through them the Vedas are made manifest all through the world . . . Like clouds gathering moisture from the ocean and pouring it down as rain for the welfare of all, the essential parts of the meaning of the Vedas were gathered and given to all in a language which everyone was qualified to know.[4]

Virtually all sects usually thought to be "Hindu" have thus, in one way or another, paid at least lip service to the notion that they are all somehow linked to the Veda and the Vedic past. The history of Hinduism, one might say, is the history of the infusion of Vedic authority, usually through simple assertion, into non-Vedic doctrines and practices. For any innovation to be "orthodox," it usually must be shown to be, in one way or another, "Vedic," that is to say, not really an innovation at all. As the prototypical source of all truth, the Veda serves as the standard for evaluating the adequacy and authority of subsequent knowledge.

This is not difficult, given a certain interpretive freedom; one may with some ease declare that virtually any of the doctrines and practices one favors are already found "in the Veda" or at least are in conformity with the wisdom of the Veda. "The Veda" was and still is a very loose term in India, and could be made to say practically anything any hermeneut wanted it to say. By representing new texts, doctrines, and practices as "already Vedic," change was both legitimated and denied, and continuity with the Vedic past was both affirmed and yet left relatively unconstraining.

This came in extremely handy in the nineteenth century when, in response to British colonialism and the challenges of the West, Hindu reform movements arose with the intention of restoring pride in Indian culture and history while at the same time legitimizing innovations and cultural borrowings. The leaders of the so-called "Neo-Hindu" movement advocated a "return to the Vedas" as the means for purifying Hinduism of its supposed later accretions and perversions. The Vedas, and particularly the Upanishads, were identified as the very essence of Hinduism. The monistic philosophy taught in some of the ancient Upanishads was regarded as the essence of "true" Hinduism and favored over the "false" forms of Hinduism that embraced polytheism and image worship. Social practices such as caste abuse, widow burning, and child marriage were opposed as "non-Vedic" in the attempt to modernize Hinduism through a return to the teachings of the ancient Vedas.

The Veda and the Vedic past were also called upon to respond to the perception that India was materially, technologically, and scientifically backward in comparison with the West. Some, like Gandhi, responded to the charge of Indian technological inferiority by turning the apparent disadvantage into an advantage: while the West may be superior in this regard, it had also been corrupted by it. Others, however, faced the problem head on and once again found their defense in the Veda. Vedic texts, according to Rāmmohan Roy (1772–1833), the founder of the neo-Hindu group known as the Brahmo Samāj, promote empiricism and reason: they "recommend mankind to direct all researches towards the surrounding objects, viewed either collectively or individually, bearing in mind their regular, wise and wonderful combinations and arrangements."[5]

Dayānanda Sarasvatī (1824–1883), the founder of the Ārya Samāj, took an even more radical tack. Since the Vedas supposedly embody the totality of all truth, the truths of modern science must already be in the Vedas. Dayānanda claimed to have found knowledge of telecommunications, capabilities for the construction of aircraft, and advanced theories of gravitational attraction already documented in Indian texts nearly three thousand years old. Vivekānanda (1863–1902), the organizer of the reformist Rāmakrishna Mission Society, also declared that sciences such as arithmetic and astronomy were already laid out in the Vedas, and that India owed nothing in this regard to Greece or the West in general.

OTHER SOURCES OF AUTHORITY FOR SACRED TEXTS

There are other sources for the authority of Hindu sacred texts besides, and in some cases superseding, the authority of the Veda. Sometimes the transcendent source of revelation is guaranteed by representing the text as the word of one or another of the Hindu deities, who may or may not also be designated as the creator of the Vedas themselves. The Puranas, for example, are usually represented as the utterances of the particular deity the sectarian text centers on, and the claim is often made that God spoke the Puranas before the Vedas.

In the Bhagavad Gita (c. 200 B.C.E.–200 C.E.), one of the most important texts of the post-Vedic Sanskritic tradition, Arjuna the warrior is instructed about sacred duty by his charioteer, Krishna (Kṛṣṇa), who turns out to be no ordinary teacher:

Though myself unborn, undying, the lord of creatures, I fashion nature, which is mine, and I come into being through my own magic. Whenever sacred duty decays and chaos prevails, then, I create myself, Arjuna. To protect men of virtue and destroy men who do evil, to set the standard of sacred duty, I appear in age after age.

—Bhagavad Gita 4.6–8[6]

God appears or takes on form (this is the doctrine of the *avatar* [*avatāra*]) in the world in times of darkness to "reassert" the "timeless" teachings of Hinduism. Once again, innovation is presented as renovation, the new is revealed under the guise of the old.

But perhaps the most powerful of the alternatives to the Veda as the source of authority for Hindu texts is the religious experience of the seer, yogic adept, mystic, saint, or holy man. A powerful strain of mysticism runs throughout the Hindu tradition that allows for the possibility of ongoing revelatory knowledge. Indeed, beginning in the texts of the Veda itself there is the alternative claim that a "higher" and mystical wisdom exists beyond the "lower" knowledge that is the Veda (*Muṇḍaka Upanishad* II.4–5).

In some instances, revelation based on experience simply replicates the paradigmatic revelation of the Vedic sages. The great Hindu epic called the *Mahabharata* represents itself as the inspired words of the semidivine and mythical seer Vyāsa, who is specifically compared to the Vedic seers. In other cases, however, human mystics and saints have claimed to have received new and authoritative insights concerning ultimate reality in the course of their own meditative or ecstatic experience, and their pronouncements take on their own independent sacrality.

Most of the sacred literature of the devotional sects of ecstatic Hinduism is comprised of the poems, songs, dramas, and musings of the poet-saints of the sects, written in the vernacular languages of India. The emptiness of formal worship, defiance of social convention, and the need for inner experience of the object of devotion (who is to be found in "one's own self") is highlighted in the following poem composed by a fourteenth-century female devotee of the god Shiva:

> I, Lalla, went out far in search of Shiva, the omnipresent Lord; after wandering, I Lalla, found Him at last within my own self, abiding in His own home.
>
> Temple and image, the two that you have fashioned, are no better than stone; the Lord is immeasurable and consists of intelligence; what is needed to realize Him is unified concentration of breath and mind.
>
> Let them blame me or praise me or adore me with flowers; I become neither joyous nor depressed, resting in myself and drunk in the nectar of the knowledge of the pure Lord.
>
> With the help of the gardeners called Mind and Love, plucking the flower called Steady Contemplation, offering the water of the flood of the Self's own bliss, worship the Lord with sacred formula of silence![7]

And in this next passage from the Hindi-speaking poet-saint Sūrdās, written in the sixteenth century, the songs composed to the deity of one's devotion (in this case Hari, another name for Vishnu) are explicitly given their own soteriological power, comparable to that of the Vedas:

> Songs to Hari work great wonders:
> They elevate the lowly of the world,
>   who celebrate their climb with drums.
> To come to the feet of the Lord in song
>   is enough to make stones float on the sea.
> No wonder that even the meanest of the mean—
>   hunters and harlots—can mount the skies,

Where wander the infinite company of the stars,
where the moon and the sun circle around,
And only Dhruv, the polestar, is fixed,
for he as a lad had sung his way to Rām.
The Vedas are verses, testaments to God—
hearing them makes the saints saintly and wise—
And what about Sūr? I sing too.
O Hari, my shelter, I've come for your care.[8]

The tradition of creating new sacred scriptures based on the experiences and declarations of Hindu saints continues. A famous recent example was Rāmakrishna (1834–1886), an illiterate priest of a Bengali temple dedicated to the goddess Kālī, who in the course of his lifetime claimed to have had many mystical experiences. Some of these entailed visions of Kālī, but others were the results of Rāmakrishna's interest in exploring the underlying essence of all world religions. His mystical experiences proving the "truth of all religions" were important for the neo-Hindu claim of universality, and his teachings were collected by his disciples under the title "The Gospel of Śrī Rāmakrishna."

WHAT ARE THE PRINCIPAL SACRED TEXTS OF HINDUISM? THE FORMS THEY TAKE

The Vedas

The Vedas are the earliest of the sacred texts of Hinduism: the earliest portion of the Rig Veda was completed by 1200 B.C.E. or before, making it also the oldest known text of the Indo-European world. Composed in Sanskrit, the Vedas are entirely centered on the performance of and speculations surrounding the cult of fire sacrifice. Each of the four Vedas consists of a Samhita ("collection" of hymns, verses, and chants), a Brahmana (*Brāhmaṇa*) (in which the mythical origins, contexts and meanings of the ritual are explained), an Aranyaka (*āraṇyaka*) ("forest text," where the more esoteric and secret significances of the rites are detailed), and an Upanishad (comprised of mystical speculations and philosophical ruminations). The Samhitas of the four Vedas (the Rig, Yajur, Sama, and Atharva) are correlated to the functions of the four main priests of the Vedic sacrifice and were composed and preserved by these priests for ritual use. Each of the four Vedas has several recensions, due to the varying practices of different ritual schools; some of these recensions have survived—completely or in fragments—and many have not.

As noted above, it is only the Veda that is accorded the status of "revelation" or shruti. All of the other sacred texts of Hinduism, no matter the esteem in which they are held, are technically classified as "traditional" or "remembered" (smriti).

The Vedangas and Sutras

The first texts of the "traditional" class are collectively known as the Vedangas (*Vedāṅgas*), or "limbs of the Veda." Composed mainly from c. 700 B.C.E. to c. 200 C.E., these works were technical treatises written in the shorthand, aphoristic form called the *sutra* (*sūtra*). The Vedangas make up the six "sciences" necessary for the correct and exact performance of the Vedic rituals: Vyākaraṇa, the study of grammar, linguistics, and philology; Nirukta, or etymology; Chaṇḍa, the explanation and practice of verse meters; Śīksa, the study of faultless pronunciation; Jyotiṣa, or the science of astronomy and astrology.

The sixth "limb of the Veda" was the Kalpa Sutras, manuals in which the rules for the actual performance of the various types of Vedic sacrifice are given. The Shrauta (Śrauta) Sutras lay out the rules for performing the most elaborate of these sacrifices, while the Gṛhya Sutras detail the protocol for executing the simpler rites of the domestic ceremonial performed by the householder himself. Also included are the Śulba Sutras, in which geometrical rules are laid out for the proper construction of the sacred space and altars of the Vedic ritual. The last component of a Kalpa Sutra (and again, different versions of these texts were composed and preserved by a variety of ritual schools) was the Dharma Sutra (also known as the Dharma Shastra [*Dharma Śāstra*]—"Teaching"—or the Dharma Smriti [*Dharma Smṛti*]). These encyclopedic texts extend the rules governing human activity previously confined to the ritual sphere to nearly every aspect of daily life, and especially concentrate on the specific and different obligations or duties (*dharma*) one has as a member of a particular social class or caste and depending on one's stage of life.

The *sutra* form was also favored by the authors of several other important texts. The Mīmāṁsā Sutras, attributed to Jaimini and dated at c. 200 B.C.E., is the root text of the philosophical school of *mīmāṃsā*, or "enquiry" into the cosmic and moral significance of the Vedic sacrifice. The Yoga Sutras of Patañjali (c. 200 B.C.E.–300 C.E. is the first systematic presentation of the practice and theory of *yoga*, or psychophysical "discipline." And the Vedānta Sutras of the great teacher Śaṅkara (c. early ninth century C.E.), which are actually commentaries on an earlier text, form the most important enunciation of the highly influential Hindu philosophical tradition known as Advaita Vedanta (Vedānta), which teaches an absolute monistic doctrine of the oneness of all being.

The Epics

Among the most popular and well-known of the Hindu scriptures are the two great epics, the *Mahabharata* and the *Ramayana*. Both of these enormous works (the *Mahabharata* is a collection of over 100,000 stanzas, the *Ramayana* about a quarter of that) were composed, in various recensions, over a period of almost a thousand years between c. 400 B.C.E. and c. 400 C.E.

Both consist of a heterogenous assortment of material—mythology, pseudo-historical lore, folktales, teachings concerning religious duty, the meaning of life, and salvation—but both also relate narratives that have come to be regarded as the backbone of the Indian cultural heritage.

The *Mahabharata* claims to be divinely inspired and all-encompassing: "Whatever is written here may also be found elsewhere; but what is not found here cannot be found anywhere else either." The text tells the story of a legendary battle for rule over India fought between two sides of the same family. After many twists and turns in the plot, the warring parties meet at the battlefield for the climactic battle. It is at this point in the story line that perhaps the single most popular Hindu text and one of the world's greatest religious works is found. The *Bhagavad Gita,* or *Song of the Lord,* is a discussion about duty and faith conducted by one of the warriors, Arjuna, and his charioteer, Krishna—who is, we learn in the course of the text, God in human form.

The *Ramayana,* attributed to the seer Valmīki, is the story of Rama (Rāma), the Prince of Ayodhya—his birth and childhood, his marriage to Sita (Sītā), his unjust banishment and exile into the wilderness, Sita's abduction by the wicked Ravana (Rāvaṇa), Rama's battle with and defeat of Ravana and the rescue of Sita, and Rama's triumphant return to Ayodhya as king. Whereas the characters in the *Mahabharata* tend to be flawed in various ways, Rama and Sita are widely regarded as ideals of obedience, loyalty, fidelity, strength, courage, and heroism.

Both of the great Hindu epics were traditionally recited by bards at the courts of kings, but were also often recited to or dramatically enacted for the masses as religious performance and popular entertainment. In recent years, both have also been made into television serials and shown on videotape, thus metamorphosing into a somewhat different kind of "sacred text."

Puranas and Other Sectarian Texts

Beginning in the early middle centuries of the common era, Sanskrit texts that codified the worldviews, doctrines, and practices of the various Hindu sects were composed. Chief among these are the Puranas ("Stories of Antiquity"). Centering on one or another of the principal deities of sectarian Hinduism—Vishnu, Shiva, or the Goddess—these texts are traditionally said to be comprised of five topics: the creation of the world, the dissolution of the world, the ages of the world, genealogies, and the history of dynasties. In actuality, however, the Puranas are as encyclopedic as the epics, replete with all sorts of myths, legends, didactic passages on religious duty and salvation, ritual instructions for temple and image worship, and tales about holy places and pilgrimage sites. Recent scholarship has indicated that most, if not all, of the Puranas were composed under the auspices of one or another ruler of particular Hindu kingdoms by priests associated with the dominant sect of the region.

Other sectarian texts are known by different names. The 108 sacred texts of the Vaishnava (Vaiṣṇava) sect known as the Pancaratras (Pāñcarātras) are designated "Samhitas" or "Agamas" (*āgamas*), certain sects worshipping the god Shiva have also produced texts called Agamas, and sects worshipping one or another form of the Goddess have composed "Tantras." These sectarian treatises are similar in content and purpose to the Puranas but tend to be more purely theological in their orientation, and they specify the particular sect's ritual practices to be followed in the temple and at home.

Devotional Texts of the Poet-Saints

While all the literature discussed above is in the language of the elite, Sanskrit, the sacred texts of what might be called "popular Hinduism" were composed in one or another of the vernacular languages of South Asia. Among the most important of these are the Tamil works of the poet-saints who served as figureheads for the devotional, and often ecstatic and emotional, movements that began in South India as early as the seventh century of the common era. Led by the devotees of Vishnu known as the Alvars (ālvārs) and the worshippers of Shiva called the Nayanmars, the devotional movement became quite popular and spread throughout India. The poems and songs of later Hindu saints of North India—Kabīr (1440–1518), Caitanya (1485–1533), Sūrdās (1485–1563), Mirabai (sixteenth century) and others—also depict the longing for God and the bliss of union with the divine in simple, yet moving terms.

LITURGICAL, INTELLECTUAL, POLITICAL, AND RITUAL USES OF SACRED TEXTS

Sacred scriptures in Hinduism are used ritually and liturgically in two principal ways: they are memorized and recited, in full or in part; and portions of them are extracted and deployed as mantras, or efficacious verbal formulas accompanying ritual actions.

Memorization and recitation of the Veda has been a critical component of upper-caste Hindu religious life since ancient times. In the idealized scheme that lays out four "stages of life," each with its distinctive set of religious duties, a young boy is given a "second birth" when he is initiated into the study of the Veda under the guidance of a teacher. This ceremony—accompanied by a bestowing of a "sacred thread," which is worn for the rest of the initiate's life—inaugurates the first stage of life: that of a religious student. For a period lasting until marriage, the boy is to dedicate himself to learning a part or even the whole of one or more of the Vedas under the careful tutelage of his *guru* who is, by virtue of his knowledge, regarded as a father or even a god:

> At the beginning and at the end of (reciting) the Veda, he should always clasp his guru's (feet) with crossed hands, touching the left

(foot) with the left (hand), and the right with the right. The guru, never tiring, should say to him as he is about to begin his recitation, "Now recite!" and he should stop him by saying, "Now stop!" He should always say, "Om!" at the beginning and end of (reciting) the Veda, for (the recitation) slips away without "Om" before it and dissolves (without "Om") after it.

—Manusmṛti 2.71–74

The man in the second stage of life, the householder, is to continue daily recitation of the Veda as part of his religiously ordained duties. In every instance, strict rules govern the recitation, specifying the proper time, place, and circumstances. The reciter should purify himself before starting and should be careful not to recite the scripture in the presence of those deemed unworthy of hearing it (i.e., primarily women and those of the lower castes). The recitation is also supposed to bring great merit—it burns away evil and demerit and helps to ensure salvation after death. Even the articulation of certain essential portions of the Veda, especially the sacred syllable *om,* is said to procure great benefits.

Some learned Brahmins to this day will demonstrate their mnemonic mastery of Veda through performances in which a text—often of great length—is chanted in incredibly intricate phonetic and melodic patterns. These Brahmins have learned the Veda literally backwards and forwards.

Following the model of Veda study and recitation, other sacred scriptures of the various Hindu traditions are similarly memorized and privately or publicly recited as part of Hindu religious life. The epics, Puranas, the *Bhagavad Gita,* and Tulsīdās's *Ramacaritamanasa,* among others, have been used in this way, and the recitation is usually also surrounded by comparable ritualized preliminaries such as ablution, special dress, and meditation. The singing or chanting of the verses of the devotionalistic poet-saints at gatherings of the faithful, recitations designed to evoke in listeners a particular religious and transformative "mood" or sentiment, and the recitations accompanied by dramatic enactments of various texts, are other examples of the high premium placed on oral recitation of sacred scripture in Hindu traditions.

The second principal ritual use of the Veda and other sacred scriptures is the employment of selected verses as mantras. Rituals of all sorts in Hinduism are punctuated with the recitation of verses or simple syllables that are believed to have special potency and help realize the desired effect of the rite. Vedic mantras are particularly efficacious. The Samhita portions of the Veda were the repository of the mantras used in the Vedic sacrificial rituals, and in post-Vedic times many of these formulas were redeployed for use in Hindu ceremonials ranging from life-cycle rites (birth, initiation, marriage, and death rituals, among others) to the rites surrounding the worship of images at home or in the temple. Consecration of sacred space—the blessing of a new home or the construction of a new temple— are inevitably accompanied by Vedic mantras. In some instances, such rituals employ mantras taken from the later scriptures of Hindu traditions, but even in post-Vedic Hinduism it is the formulas from the Veda that are favored.

Mantras are also used as mediational aids. Initiation into one or another of the sects of Hinduism often entails the imparting of a special, sometimes secret, mantra to the initiate by the guru. This mantra is to be repeated over and over again, in part because of its supposed intrinsic power and in part to help focus the mind. Yogic traditions have often relied on what are called "seed mantras"—monosyllabic words without ordinary language meaning that are thought to capture the essence of parts or the whole of the cosmos—to instill special powers into the practitioner and to provide a vehicle for the "one-pointedness of mind" that is the goal of yoga. Repetition of the name of God in certain devotional sects serves a similar purpose, focussing the devotee's attention on the object of his or her devotion. Another purpose of this kind of mantra is to provide a kind of nucleus for philosophical reflection. The sacred syllable *om* is said to be the very sound of the universe as a whole, thereby providing an oral representation of the philosophical teachings of monistic Advaita Vedanta.

Hindu philosophers of different schools have tended to gravitate toward certain sacred scriptures, such as the Upanishads and the *Bhagavad Gita,* where they find evidence for their particular perspectives. These texts can be and have been read in quite different ways for their philosophical content; they have been interpreted as proof texts not only for the Advaita Vedanta position of absolute undifferentiated monism but also for schools of theistically infused "qualified monism" led by Rāmānuja (1025–1137) and Madhva (1238–1317). The philosophical teachings of "Neo-Vedanta" so typical of the reformers of the nineteenth and twentieth centuries also depended on the Upanishads, which were regarded as the pinnacle of Hindu spirituality and thought.

In addition to these ritual, meditative, and philosophical uses of sacred texts, some scriptures have also been put to more worldly purposes. The Dharma Sutras or Shastras have since ancient times functioned as the basis for legal codes, a practice that was continued under the British rule of India in the nineteenth and early twentieth centuries, when the personal law governing members of Hindu communities was based on these texts. The Dharma Sutras, together with parts of the epics and Puranas, have also been employed as guides for the proper rulership of Hindu kings and have often been cited to buttress the caste system and the ideology of social inequality.

Some sacred texts—especially the Puranas—were apparently composed originally to help legitimate the political rulership of particular Hindu kings and dynasties. The political use of scripture was probably already a feature of Vedic life, as rulers and priests colluded to justify their privileged positions, and continues right through Indian history to the present. A recent movement of Hindu nationalists sometimes cites the Veda, epics, and other texts as charters for a hoped-for transformation of the modern and secular nation-state of India into a religiously oriented Hindu nation. The *Ramayana* in particular has been cited to buttress claims to disputed sacred space and to provide ancient and sacred models of Hindu leadership.

Religion and politics have always gone hand in hand, but in the late twentieth century the fusion of the two is especially apparent in India as elsewhere. While Hindu sacred texts continue to be used in a variety of ways by ordinary Hindus, they are also being drafted into the service of those who oppose secularism, harbor resentment against "outsiders" (Westerners as well as indigenous Muslims), and wish to institute "the rule of God" (*rām rājya*) in modern India.

CHAPTER 5

Christianity

HOW DOES CHRISTIANITY MAKE ITS ENDURING STATEMENTS? WHAT EXACTLY DOES CHRISTIANITY MEAN BY A TEXT?

The term "text" naturally brings to mind the image of a written source, a form of words that stays the same, although the understanding of those words may change. During the modern period, Americans have commonly thought of authority as deriving from texts, whether from the Constitution of the United States or from the Bible of the Old and New Testaments. The result has been a growing legalism in the fields of both politics and religion. It is no coincidence that our society, which in global history must rank as the most devoted to legal proceedings, is also the most prone to the idea that the whole of a religion can be conveyed by its books.

In order for us to appreciate how authority is developed within the church, we need to be clear in our minds that the "texts" of Christianity are not only—and not even primarily—written. Perhaps it is best to begin to explain this by referring to an important event in publishing within Christianity (and the modern history of the West). In 1516, Erasmus of Rotterdam brought out an edition of the New Testament that was to prove seminal during the Reformation of the sixteenth century. It was the first printed version in Greek, which permitted scholars to go behind the Latin translation of their time, and to render the original documents into their own native languages.

Now the publication of any book is obviously a textual event. Particularly, what Erasmus did—along with the work of other scholars, translators, and liturgists—made it possible for a tremendous wealth of tradition to be made available in a published form. The Reformation represented a textualizing of Christianity, and it gave a powerful incentive to movements toward general literacy and private interpretation, which were certainly not generally encouraged during the Middle Ages.

But Erasmus named his Greek New Testament something strange. Following the usage of Tertullian during the second century, he gave it the title *Novum Instrumentum*—"new instrument." I once asked a professor at my theological seminary why Erasmus had done that, and he replied, "Erasmus liked to surprise people." Historically, that was a good answer. But something else lies behind the choice Erasmus made. An "instrument" is not a static object: it is a tool and a vehicle that is to be used for a purpose. Erasmus already had changes in mind for the church, as his famous book *The Praise of Folly* clearly shows. But his Greek Testament was not an "instrument" because he personally intended to use it for something, but because it was an instrument of the purposes of God.

The New Testament becomes an instrument for the church in the sense that it offers guidance from God. There is no sense in which that text is seen as the only way God is present to people of God. In volume one of The Pilgrim Library of World Religions, we have already learned that Christianity understands that individuals, by means of their own spirit, may through Jesus Christ become aware of and be informed by the Spirit of God. That fundamental conception of the Divine and of how the Divine becomes available has never been abandoned in the history of the church.

But at the same time, the church as a social entity must confront a problem (both potential and actual) that is every bit as fundamental as its conception of God. What happens when two or more people, imbued by the Spirit of God through Christ, disagree profoundly? God is known spiritually by each of those people, and the very fact of the creation of the world shows that divine authority must take precedence over any created power, including human authority. So if partners to a dispute both claim spiritual authority, the potential for profound and violent disagreement is obvious. The history of the church illustrates how that violent potential may be realized unless there is some way of coordinating equal claims to the Spirit of God that very different individuals may insist upon.

Within the New Testament itself, there are powerful indications that the problems of division were felt acutely within the primitive church. In a passage from his first letter to the Corinthians, written around 55 C.E., Paul spelled out the reality of deep divisions within the congregation at Corinth and his own reaction to that situation:

> It has been made clear to me, my brothers, by Chloe's people, that there are contentions among you. I mean this: each of you says, "I am Paul's," and "I am Apollos'," and "I am Cephas'," and "I am Christ's." Has Christ been divided up? Paul was not crucified for you!—Or were you baptized into Paul's name?!
>
> —1 Corinthians 1:11–12

The obvious anger of Paul's response is rooted in what he takes to be an offense against the very nature of Christ by such divisions as are evident in Corinth. "Has Christ been divided up?" is a rhetorical question, designed to affirm that Christ is in fact a principle of social unity, not simply what a series of individuals make of Christ.

It is not surprising that Paul assumes his readers will readily accept his insistence upon the principle of the unity of Christ. It is also expressed, in the name of the risen Jesus, at the close of the Gospel according to Matthew. That Gospel was probably composed in a form in which we would easily recognize it around the year 80 C.E., but its primary materials were for the most part available during the time of Paul. At the close of that Gospel, Jesus' final words are, "And behold, I am with you all days, until the completion of the age" (Matthew 28:20). That promise is a continuation of Jesus' earlier affirmation, that "Where two or three are gathered together in my name, there I am in the midst of them" (18:20). Jesus' presence is guaranteed, provided those two or three are in prayerful agreement (see 18:19).

This promise of Jesus' presence is obviously linked to the fact of gathering in his name, and it is of interest that the term used here in Matthew 18:20 for "gathered together" (*sunegmenoi*) is related to the term for "synagogue" (*synagoge*), used in the sense of a communal meeting. Because Jesus is understood to mediate the divine presence, meeting in Jesus' name as well as in the Father's power is taken to effect a communal empowerment. The two verses immediately preceding Matthew 18:20 make the stress on this understanding of this empowerment unmistakably clear:

> Truly I say to you, whatever you bind upon the earth will have been bound in heaven, and whatever you loose upon earth will have been loosed in heaven. Again I say to you, If two of you agree upon earth in regard to any matters which they pray about, it will be done for them by my Father in heaven.
>
> —Matthew 18:18–19

Now it becomes plain that meeting and agreeing in the environment of Jesus' name is also meeting and agreeing in the environment of heaven. It is the very opposite of the dissension

Paul complains about: agreement in Christ is held to bring with it the endorsement of divine power.

Within Christianity, authority derives from the power of God as exercised within the congregation, the synagogue gathered in the name of Christ. The "texts" of Christianity are truly instruments, means by which the integrity of that gathering as an encounter in the environment of Christ's presence may be assured. Four basic instruments of the spiritual integrity of the church have been recognized, usually as articulated by Irenaeus, bishop of Lyons (in modern-day France) during the second century. The first and most obvious of these is the Scripture, understood as the Bible of Israel and the writings of the New Testament as read throughout the church. The second is what Irenaeus called "the rule of faith," that is, the ongoing expression of belief on the basis of the tradition handed on by the apostles of Jesus. The third instrument of the social integrity of Christianity is sacramental identity, the prayerful dedication in common to baptism and eucharist. Finally, the fourth instrument is the apostolic ministry of the church, its commitment to principles and practices of leadership endorsed from the time Jesus first sent out a select group of his disciples to represent himself and his activity.

Each of these instruments, the "texts" of authority in the church, has been variously understood over the course of Christian history, often to the point of contention, division, and violence. But there is also a fundamental consensus that they are the appropriate point of departure for any understanding of authority within the church.

WHAT ARE THE PRINCIPAL SACRED TEXTSOF CHRISTIANITY? THE FORMS THEY TAKE

Scripture

The basic attitude toward the Old Testament and the New Testament within Christianity has already been set out in the statement of the "sources" of the various religions discussed in these volumes. Here we need to understand the authority of Scripture more specifically, and Irenaeus remains our best guide. He deliberately emphasizes the place of the Hebrew Bible within Christian Scripture, and that is the appropriate point of departure for appreciating his orientation as a whole.

He did so in opposition to groups within the church that were called Gnostic. We may describe Gnosticism as a movement that claimed that knowledge (*gnosis*) held the secret to an existence of pure spirit, outside the constraints of human flesh. Marcion was among the most prominent of Gnostic teachers. He came from Asia Minor to Rome and founded his own community there during the middle of the second century. He claimed that the God of Jesus was different from the God of the Jews, and repudiated the use of the Hebrew Bible. Because the Scriptures of Israel feature prominently within the documents of the New Testament, Marcion also rejected the majority of the New Testament writings. His collection of acceptable works included only Luke's Gospel and ten letters of Paul; even then, Marcion expunged what he considered to be Jewish additions to the texts.

Another second-century immigrant to Rome (this time from Egypt), named Valentinus, was also a Gnostic. He was not the organizer Marcion was, but his teaching was very influential. He represents the wing of Gnosticism that was concerned with the existence of the present, evil world: How could it derive from God, who is truly good? Valentinus argued that the Father is transcendent, quite apart from and other than what we can see around us. The world came into existence after a series of quasi-divine beings were generated from the Father; the last of these was Wisdom. Wisdom desired to find her way back to the Father, but her ignorance led to her spirit being imprisoned in matter. Such, according to Valentinus, is the predicament of spiritual people, who are trapped in the false world of matter, and only knowledge of the Father can save them.

Schemes of this kind may seem abstract and complicated, but they enjoyed a tremendous appeal during the second century. For all their complexity, they offered a theological account of the very human feeling of being trapped in an evil world, far from a remote spiritual home.

The early church tolerated—and openly encouraged—a great deal of variety, but teachers such as Marcion and Valentinus appeared to Irenaeus to remove too much of the God and the Scriptures of Israel, and to insist too much on their own, specialist readings of the New Testament. He insisted in opposition to the Gnostics, in a work called *Against Heresies*, that the Father of Jesus is also the God who created the world in which we live. But Irenaeus' point was not in any way that this God should be thought of as being tainted with the obvious imperfections and evils in life as we know it. Rather, he saw Christ as *recapitulating* the experience of humanity from the moment of the first man's sin. By "recapitulation," Irenaeus meant that Christ takes up all of biblical history and brings it to its fruition, when people can again live fully in the image and likeness of God. The purpose of creation as attested in Israel's Scripture (see Genesis 1:26–27) is attained in Christ. As Irenaeus was fond of saying, "God became man that man might become divine" (*Against Heresies* 3.10.2; 3.19.1; 4.33.4, 11).

The Rule of Faith

Because Gnostics genuinely were expert in interpretation, to assert the authority of the Scriptures, even of the Scriptures of Israel, was not an adequate response to their teaching. After all, Gnostics were known to make the statement of God in Isaiah 45:7, "Forming light and creating darkness, making peace and creating evil, I am the LORD, doing all these things," into an accusation: was that not an open admission of imperfection? Alongside more strictly textual authority, Irenaeus cited the rule of faith.

The rule of faith was not a fixed form of belief, but an appeal to the consensus of the church from the time of the Apostles. The point was not that the church preserved the teaching of the Apostles unchanged, but that the church taught in a conscious and substantial line of succession from the Apostles. Irenaeus insisted that faith was not simply a matter of private opinion, but a conviction through the whole of the church. Such faith was "catholic," which means "through the whole" (*kath holou*). It was as you might find it in Alexandria, Lyons, Rome, Corinth, Antioch, or wherever. Catholic Christianity was designed to avoid any particular requirement being made upon Christians.

The twin principles of the rule of faith, apostolicity and catholicity, in fact determined discussion of the actual contents of the Bible. There were many works available in the early history of the church, involving private revelation and ornate argument and creative narrative. Some of those works were widely appreciated, but the principles of catholicity and apostolicity were applied during the course of a long discussion (which lasted into the fourth century of the common era) in order to determine which documents could be used in the regular worship of the church at large. Taken together, they amounted to a standard or "canon" (from the Greek term *kanon*), a publishable measure of how the church as a whole, catholic in its range and apostolic in its origin, might practice and develop its faith.

The rule of faith, especially in its opposition to Gnosticism, came emphatically to insist upon the Incarnation as a central aspect of belief in God. "Incarnation" is a concept derived from the conviction that, in Jesus Christ, the word of God "became flesh (in Latin, *caro*) and dwelt among us" (John 1:14). The incarnational emphasis of catholic Christianity is accurately conveyed by its creed, which is still in use under the title The Apostles' Creed:

I believe in God the Father almighty,
    maker of heaven and earth,
and in Jesus Christ, his only Son, our Lord
    who was conceived by the Holy Spirit,
    born of the virgin Mary,
    suffered under Pontius Pilate,
    was crucified, dead, and buried.
    He descended into hell;
    the third day he rose from the dead,
    and ascended into heaven,
    and sits at the right hand of God the Father almighty.
    From there he is to come to judge the living and the dead.
I believe in the Holy Spirit,
    the holy catholic Church,
    the communion of saints,
    the forgiveness of sins,
    the resurrection of the body,
    and the life everlasting. Amen.

The division of the creed into three sections—corresponding to Father, Son, and Spirit—is evident. That marks the commitment of catholic Christianity to the Trinity as a means of conceiving God. Indeed, that conception correlates with the kind of incarnational faith which is expressed in the creed.

The Incarnation refers principally to Jesus as the embodiment of God, from the time of the prologue of John's Gospel (1:1–18). In the creed, however, that view of the Incarnation is developed further. The longest, middle paragraph shows that the ancient practice of Christian instruction prior to baptism (catechesis) is at the heart of the creed. That paragraph is a fine summary of the Gospels (and compare Peter's speech in Acts 10:34–43). Its level of detail articulates a rigorous alternative to the tendency of Gnosticism toward abstraction. But the statement about Jesus does not stand on its own. His status as Son is rooted in the Father's creation of the heavens and the earth. The creed begins with an embrace of the God of Israel as creator and with an equally emphatic (if indirect) rejection of any dualism that would remove God from the realities of our world.

The last paragraph of the creed, devoted to the Holy Spirit, also recollects the catechesis of Christians, which climaxed with baptism and reception of the Spirit. That basic understanding was rooted in the catechesis of Peter (again, see Acts 10:34–43, and the sequel in vv. 44–48). But here the common reception by Christians of the Spirit is used to assert the communal nature of life in the Spirit. To be baptized is to share the Spirit with the catholic church: that is where communion with God and forgiveness are to be found.

Finally, the creed closes on a deeply personal and existential note: "The resurrection of the body" does not refer to Jesus' Resurrection (which has already been mentioned in the preceding paragraph of the creed), but to the ultimate aspiration of all who believe in him. The creed does not spell out its understanding of how God raised Jesus and is to raise us from the dead, but it is unequivocal that we are all to be raised as ourselves, as embodied personality. (Paul's understanding of the body and spirit, which is basic to the creed, has already been discussed in volume one of The Pilgrim Library of World Religions). There is no trace here of joining an undifferentiated divine entity, or of some part of us (a soul, an essence) surviving in a disembodied way. That is because the creed embodies the rule of faith: the catholic and apostolic roots of the conviction that God in Christ was in the process of reconciling the world to God's self (so Paul in 2 Corinthians 5:19).

The Sacraments of Baptism and Eucharist

Once one understands, looking at the world around us through the eyes of faith, that God is actively transforming us and those around us according to his purposes, there is a potential that any person, any event or thing, might convey the presence of God to us. In that sense, there is no limit to the number of sacraments we might imagine, because sacraments are classically understood from the time of Augustine as an outward and visible sign of an inward and spiritual grace. The Christian perspective on the world is inherently sacramental.

The term *sacramentum* in Latin actually means "oath" or "vow." In secular Latin, the term can even refer to the money one deposits to provide surety of one's word. Jesus had promised his disciples, "Where two or three are gathered together in my name, there I am in the midst of them" (Matthew 18:20). Sacraments keep that promise. More strictly understood, the sacraments are occasions of worship when God presents God's self in the actual objects that are involved—in the things done and said.

Christians have differed, often sharply, over the number of sacraments that should be understood to involve this public presence of God in the pragmatics of worship. During the Middle Ages, Hugh of St. Victor enumerated a long series of sacraments, which related to one's religious experience within natural law, written law, and grace. Later, Martin Luther counted only three (baptism, eucharist, and penance). In the midst of the controversies of the Reformation, the Council of Trent in 1547 established seven sacraments as the doctrine of the Roman Catholic church, although that number had long been tradtional.

But whatever the number fixed upon, baptism and eucharist stand out within any sacramental theology. Here there is always a physical mediation of the presence and action of God within the worship of the church: by means of water in baptism, by means of bread and wine in eucharist. The other five sacraments depend on the prior acceptance of baptism and/or eucharist. At confirmation, one accepts the faith involved in baptism; in penance, one attains the forgiveness one needs to participate in

eucharist, the Lord's meal of fellowship. Marriage is the establishment of a covenant between two people that draws its spiritual strength from our relationship to God through Christ, and
unction (anointing at the point of death) commends us to our
Maker on the basis of that relationship. Holy orders establish
the role of certain individuals to serve the church as leaders.

Because baptism and eucharist are the fundamental sacraments of the church, we will focus our attention on them. Of
course, discussion and debate and disagreement have attended
any attempt to explain how these principal sacraments work.
Differences among the many denominations of the church are
typically spelled out in sacramental terms: what the sacraments
basically are, as well as how many there are. It is not possible
here even to enumerate the basic issues in play within that contention, because they are differently understood by different
churches. In any case, our purpose is not to understand why
Christians fall out with one another, but to see what the underlying, sacramental impulse is that drives them all. For that reason, we will turn to Paul's view of baptism and eucharist.
Although he was himself a controversial figure within primitive
Christianity, Paul represents a broad consensus of the church of
his time in sacramental terms. And up until today, practically
no Christian would deny the Pauline explanation of the sacraments, whatever additional explanations may be embraced.

In his letter to the Romans, written around the year 57 C.E.
Paul explains baptism as the fundamental sacrament of Christian identity:

Don't you know that as many of us as were baptized into Christ
were baptized into his death? We then were buried with him
through baptism, into death, so that just as Christ was raised from
the dead through the glory of the Father, so we also might walk in
newness of life.

—Romans 6:3–4

The assumption here is that, as was typical within the practice of the church, baptism was a liturgical event associated with Easter, in which the congregation saw the baptisand enter the water and emerge, heard the baptisand call on God as Father on emerging from the water, and connected these events with a recitation of the story of Jesus' passion—his suffering, execution, and Resurrection.

One's identification with Christ in baptism, in other words, was and is a fundamental conviction of Christian faith. Elsewhere, in his earlier letter to the Galatians (composed around the year 53 C.E.), Paul even portrays believers using the Aramaic term *'Abba* in order to call upon God under the influence of the baptismal Spirit (Galatians 4:6, discussed in volume one of The Pilgrim Library of World Religions). The principal reason for which the earliest Christians recollected Jesus was not historical curiosity, but the desire to know the image of God in human form, which was their identity in baptism.

The "newness of life" to which Paul refers in the passage from Romans is both immediate and definitive. In the short term, sin is no longer to reign in our mortal body, and the members of our body are no longer to be used for the purposes of evil; we rather are to present ourselves physically to God, as those risen from the dead, and to act for the sake of God's justice (Romans 6:12–13). That change is not just a matter of trying to do right. The ethical point of baptism is that we become new people, who have accepted the identity God wills us in Christ, and the false identity imposed on us by a sinful world is washed away. In the ultimate term, "If we have become joined in growth with the likeness of his death, nonetheless we will be also with the Resurrection" (Romans 6:5). The polarity of Christ's death and Resurrection is the setting in which baptism occurs, and the event itself moves the believer through that polarity to an existence characterized by righteousness in the present and eternal life in the future.

As baptism is the event in which one appropriates one's divine identity in Christ, eucharist is the communal occasion during which the community as a whole celebrates that identity. The term *eukharistia* in Greek means "thanksgiving," and it became the preferred term, during and after the period of the New Testament, for what Paul himself calls "the Lord's supper." Much later, Catholics and Protestants divided over whether to call the sacrament "mass" or "communion." "Mass" derives from the last words of the Latin liturgy, *Ite, missa est*—"Depart, it is ended"—while "Communion" refers to the fellowship of participants with Christ and one another.

Paul is as succinct and clear about eucharist as he is about baptism:

> The cup of blessing which we bless, is it not participation in the blood of Christ? The bread which we break, is it not participation in the body of Christ? Because there is one bread, we are one body, although we are many, because we all share from the one bread.
> —1 Corinthians 10:16–17

Paul goes on in his letters to develop in many ways the insight that believers are joined into a single body, and later writings in his name were to articulate the motif even further. But in the passage just cited, Paul shows us both the origin and the direction of his understanding of "the body of Christ." It begins with the theology of eucharist, in which consuming the bread identifies the believer with Christ's death, and it consummates in the declaration that all who share that bread are incorporated into Christ, as into a single body.

Paul refers to this sharing of identity as "participation" or "fellowship," *koinonia* in Greek. It refers to what is held in common (*koinos*) and mutual, as well as to what is basic. The thanksgiving meal for Paul is founded on a celebration by ordinary elements, wine and bread shared among those baptized into Christ, which deepens the participants' identity by their joining with one another. They now possess the strength and coherence of a single "body."

The transition to this idea of the body was natural for Paul, because he was familiar with the Hellenistic conception of corporate "body," which was especially popularized by Stoic writers. Seneca, the philosopher and tutor of Nero, wrote of the world as a whole, "All of this which you see, in which the human and the divine is included, is one; we are members of a great body" (*Moral Letters* 95.52). For Paul, "The body of Christ" is no mere metaphor, but describes the living solidarity of those who share the Spirit of God by means of baptism and eucharist.

Paul is the best commentator on his own thought. He explains in a fairly predictable way how diverse members belong to a single body in 1 Corinthians 12, just after he has treated of the eucharist. In the midst of that discussion, he puts forward the "body of Christ" as the principal definition of the church:

> For just as the body is one and has many members, and all the members of the body (being many) are one body, so is Christ. For by one Spirit we were all baptized into one body—whether Jews or Greeks, slave or free—and we all were given to drink of one Spirit.
>
> —1 Corinthians 12:12–13

By focusing on the "body" as the medium of eucharistic solidarity and then developing its corporate meaning, Paul turns the traditional understanding of Spirit (as received in baptism) into the single principle of Christian identity. His reply to any attempt to form discrete fellowships within the church will now always be, "Is Christ divided?" (so 1 Corinthians 1:13). The principle of a spiritual unity, celebrated and enhanced by means of eucharist, is basic within the Christian practice of worship.

Both baptism and eucharist, then, involve the inward grace of one's identity with God through Christ as well as the outward instruments of water in baptism and wine and bread in eucharist. Baptism bestows identity, and eucharist celebrates that identity. To some extent, the difference between the two is a matter of the emotions. Baptism is a touching and a sobering occasion, particularly when an infant is baptized, because it is the moment when we recognize our mortality, and dedicate that part of us to the pattern of Jesus' death. Of course, as we have seen, death here is understood to be the first element in a polarity that includes resurrection, but the fact of our human nature, when recognized, brings with it a feeling of vulnerability and some loneliness. But we say that eucharist is "celebrated," because it is a matter of sharing and enhancing a common identity whose end is eternal life. There is an anticipation in every eucharist of the full heritage that is presently enjoyed, but not yet complete, and often a particular—and joyful—remembrance of those who have died. After all, eucharist—most often celebrated on Sunday, God's day—brings us all into the presence of the living Christ, who is ever ready to be present in our midst.

Apostolic Ministry

The term "apostle" (from the Greek *apostolos*) means "someone who has been sent, commissioned for a purpose." Jesus' action of sending some of his followers away from him in order to engage in the same sort of activity that he did distinguishes him from other rabbis of his period. At the same time, his commissioning of the twelve apostles—known as the Twelve, and corresponding to the twelve tribes of Israel—establishes the underlying structure and function of Christian ministry.

Discussion of the source known as Q has brought about a remarkable consensus that at least some of the sayings within it were circulated a few years after the crucifixion, around the year

35 C.E. Recent study includes in the earliest version of Q the charge to Jesus' specially commissioned disciples (Luke 10:3–11, 16), a strategy to cope with resistance to their message (Luke 6:27–35), examples of how to speak of God's kingdom (Luke 6:20b–21; 11:2–4, 14–20; 13:18–21), curses to lay on those who reject those sent in the name of the kingdom (Luke 11:39–48, 52), and a section relating John the Baptist and Jesus as principal emissaries of God's kingdom (Luke 7:24b–28a, 33–34).

At the start of the tradition called Q, Jesus' teaching was arranged in the form of a mishnah by his disciples. In fact, one of the few things we can say about Q is that it was not originally called Q, as it is in modern discussion. That letter is an abbreviation for the German term *Quelle*, which means "source," and the assumption is often that it was a written document. Obviously, no one knows whether we are dealing with written or oral material; all anyone knows is that there are about 200 verses, mostly sayings of Jesus, that Matthew and Luke share, and that are mostly absent from Mark.

This material seems to reflect the disciples' organization of the sayings of Jesus into a mishnah that they could repeat. They took up a ministry in Jesus' name, which was addressed to Israel at large after the Resurrection. The mishnaic form of Q was preserved orally in Aramaic, and it explained how the Twelve were to discharge their mission. It included just the materials that have already been specified, instructions to Jesus' disciples, a strategy of love to overcome resistance, paradigms to illustrate the kingdom of God, threats directed toward enemies, and a reference to John the Baptist, which would serve as a transition to baptism in the name of Jesus. As specified, that is probably the original, mishnaic order of Q. It is the order that accords with the purpose of the Twelve within the mission to Israel.

Apostolic ministry finds its purpose when it is understood in terms of the kingdom of God, which was the central focus of Jesus' own ministry. What these disciples are told to do seems strange, unless the image of the harvest at the beginning of the charge to them (Luke 10:2) is taken seriously. Because they are going out as to rich fields, they do not require what would normally be required on a journey: purse, bag, and sandals are dispensed with (Luke 10:4). They are to treat Israel as a field in which one works, not as an itinerary of travel; greeting people along the way (which would only lead to diversions from the task) is even proscribed in Luke 10:4.

In addition, staffs are also prohibited, although they were normally used on journeys for support and protection. That is a detail that we actually know from Luke 9:3, and shows that another, powerful analogy is at work within the commission of the Twelve. The Mishnah reflects the common practice in Jerusalem of prohibiting pilgrims from entering the Temple with the bags and staffs and purses that they had traveled with (Berakhoth 9:5). All such items were to be deposited prior to worship, so that one was present simply as a representative of Israel. Part of worship was that one was to appear in one's simple purity. The issue of purity also figures prominently in the charge to the disciples (although it is overlooked far too often).

The very next injunction (Luke 10:5–8) instructs the disciples to enter into any house of a village they enter, and to offer their peace. They are to accept hospitality in that house, eating what is set before them. The emphasis upon eating what is provided is repeated (Luke 10:7, 8), so that it does not appear to be a later, marginal elaboration. On the other hand, the number of seventy disciples, given in Luke 10:1, is probably a later addition to the mishnaic Q. Seventy was the traditional number of all the nations in Judaism, and it became symbolic of the universal mission of the church after the Resurrection.

Jesus' insistence that his disciples accept hospitality in whatever house would accept him is fully consonant with his reputation as a "glutton and a drunkard" (see Matthew 11:19 and Luke 7:34). There is a deliberate carelessness involved, in the precise sense that the disciples are not to have a care in regard to the practices of purity of those who offer hospitality to them. Those people are true Israelites. When they join in the meals of the kingdom that Jesus' disciples have arrived to celebrate, when they accept and grant forgiveness to one another in the manner of the Lord's Prayer, what they set upon the table of fellowship from their own effort is by definition pure, and should be gratefully consumed. The twelve disciples define and create the true Israel to which they are sent, and they tread that territory as on holy ground, shoeless, without staff or purse. At the close of the charge, the disciples are instructed to shake the dust off their feet from any place that does not receive them (Luke 10:11).

That gesture is, of course, vivid on any reading. But on the understanding of the charge that we have developed here, the symbolism is particularly acute. Towns that do not receive the disciples have cut themselves off from the kingdom of God, and can expect worse than what was in store for Sodom (Luke 10:11–12).

The activities of the disciples in the fellowship of Israel are essentially to be the activities of Jesus. As Luke presents Q, they are to heal the sick and preach that the kingdom has drawn near (Luke 10:9); as Matthew presents Q, they are to preach that the kingdom has drawn near and heal, raise the dead, cleanse lepers, and cast out demons, all the while taking and giving freely (Matthew 10:7–8). Taken as a whole, Jesus' charge of the disciples at the mishnaic stage of Q is an enacted parable of the kingdom of God. The fact that the kingdom has drawn near is the foundation of everything that is commanded, and the disciples are to address the people they gather in towns and villages in order to announce that dawning reality. Their preaching in itself is a witness to the nature of Jesus' teaching of the kingdom of God, as the near and definitive reality that conditions all of truly human life.

LITURGICAL, INTELLECTUAL, POLITICAL, AND RITUAL USES OF SACRED TEXTS

The deep principles of Scripture, the rule of faith, sacraments, and apostolic ministry are related to distinct traditions and different structures of authority in the various denominations of the church. To try to indicate them all, whether in history or simply within the contemporary scene, would involve an enormous catalog. To attempt to evaluate one structure of authority in comparison to others (for instance, to assess the Protestant emphasis on the authority of Scripture) would be unfair here, because that would involve a specifically theological argument.

For example, both the Roman Catholic church and many Pentecostal churches claim a uniquely apostolic authority. The claims of Rome are founded on Jesus' promise to Peter in Matthew 16:18–19, taken as warranting the institution of the papacy. The claims of Pentecostalists are founded on Acts 2:1–42, where the same Peter explains the mighty events of Pentecost in terms of God pouring out his Spirit through Jesus on the gathered congregation. Obviously, those two understandings involve different and contradictory views of how Scripture attests the operation of divine authority and of how apostolic ministry is actualized. But the appeal to Scripture and apostolicity as indispensable instruments of God's will is common to Catholics and Pentecostalists, as it is to Christians generally, while the rule of faith and the sacraments (however they are counted) also take their place as instruments of authority throughout the church.

Rather than attempting to trace the (functionally endless) varieties of denominational understandings, we will close with four clear instances in recent history in which the four underlying instruments of divine authority have been invoked within the church in order to provide leadership. Not every person about to be mentioned would be claimed as a hero of faith by all Christians, and in some cases perhaps even a majority of Christians would express reservations about the behavior involved. But each of the four has been recognized in his own time and later to have provided a fresh understanding of what and how the church should be.

Intellect and Scripture: The Case of Dietrich Bonhoeffer

In 1943, Bonhoeffer, a Lutheran pastor, was arrested for his part in a conspiracy to assassinate Adolf Hitler. He had long courted danger by his resistance to the Third Reich and his support of the Confessing Church in Germany (that is, those Christians who refused to accept the control of the Nazis). After the plot failed, Bonhoeffer was hanged, along with five thousand other people, in 1945. Both his vigorous opposition to the Third Reich and his refusal to stay abroad in Britain or the United States (where he was enthusiastically embraced as a fine theologian), make him a striking figure.

In his *Ethics*, later published from fragments he was able to write in prison, Bonhoeffer revealed the source of his unusual choices. Lutheran theology, as he was well aware, had long embraced the principle clearly articulated by Paul that legitimate authority was to be accepted as instituted by God (see Romans 13:1–7). But the situation of his world made it obvious that the available institutions had failed: "The social, economic, political and other problems of the world have become too much for us; all the available offers of ideological and practical solutions are inadequate."[1] Bonhoeffer specifically included the church in his analysis: "She has given offence, so that men are prevented from believing her message."

Bonhoeffer offered a radically biblical response to the confusion of his time. No institution, no matter how important, could be set alongside the single authority of Jesus Christ as the word of God:

It is in Jesus Christ that God's relation to the world is defined. We know of no relation of God to the world other than through Jesus Christ. . . . In other words, the proper relation of the Church to the world cannot be deduced from natural law or rational law or from universal human rights, but *only* from the gospel of Jesus Christ.[2]

Bonhoeffer appealed to the opening of John's Gospel (1:1–18) as the classic "word of the incarnation of God, of the love of God for the world in the sending of his Son," so all speech and all action should accept that single standard of judgment. No other institution, no matter how venerable or powerful, could claim primacy in comparison to that. By the end of his life, Bonhoeffer's theology and his militant opposition to National Socialism were coordinated by means of his reading of Scripture.

The Rule of Faith in Liturgy: The Case of Angelo Roncalli

Roncalli is better known as Pope John XXIII, and as such may stand as the greatest reformer in the modern history of Roman Catholicism. Soon after his election in 1958, he called the Second Vatican Council (Vatican II), making it clear that he wished the work of renewal to be undertaken by the bishops assembled, rather than by the court of the Pope himself. Despite opposition, the Council opened in 1962, and John announced himself satisfied with the work of updating (*aggiornamento*) when that first session closed. He convened the second session for the following year, but he died of cancer on 3 June 1963, before the session convened.

Despite the brevity of his pontificate and continuing disputes concerning the meaning of Vatican II, in one regard there can be no question of the impact of John XXIII. The Council accepted that the mass and other sacraments should be made available in the actual language of the people who participate, rather than in Latin. Moreover, the report on liturgy also allowed that local variation, rather than rigid uniformity, should be admitted and encouraged in the development of worship. Both those principles, associated with Protestantism since the sixteenth century, entered the Catholic tradition with John's endorsement.

In this case, the rule of faith, which had long been discussed by Catholic theologians and pastors and lay people, was able to articulate itself afresh in new circumstances by means of papal encouragement. The purpose, of course, was not in any way to diminish "the divine Eucharistic sacrifice," but to make it even more vivid as "the outstanding means by which the faithful can express in their lives, and manifest to others, the mystery of Christ and the real nature of the true church."[3] In this very clear statement, the Council made it clear that it was not adopting a Protestant emphasis on the individual's understanding of the faith, but was enhancing its dedication to a sacramental definition of the church.

Radical Sacraments: The Case of Daniel Berrigan

Berrigan, a Jesuit priest, was taken into custody in 1970, in order to serve his sentence for a crime he committed in 1968. In Catonsville, Maryland, he had participated in the destruction of draft records, a blatant breach of United States federal law. During the period in which he was a fugitive, he taped a sermon for the chaplaincy of Smith College. His moral foundation is succinctly expressed:

> I would not have any child born into this world, into this nation, into this church, in order to bear arms, in order to belong to the stratagems of death, in order to obey the Pentagon, in order to raven the poor in distant lands, to die there, to kill there, in any sense, in any case, to perish there, as man.[4]

"Death," for Berrigan here, is not simply one's mortal fate, but a spiritual power opposed to Christ.

Berrigan's own stratagem to resist is couched in sacramental terms; he seeks to observe and replicate the saving act of Jesus:

> That is where you saw, as we say in the ancient creed, "He was crucified, died, and was buried"—which is to say he submitted before the imperial power that claimed his life. He preferred to suffer violence in his person rather than to inflict it on others. He died a criminal, his body placed in a tomb. He was shoveled into the inert grave. Or as we say in the Resistance, he acted and went underground, and some days later when it was expedient for others, he surfaced again, and with great pains, identified himself as the One of the Friday we call Good.
>
> I am struck by all this as an exemplary action and passion for ourselves. That is to say that Jesus, by a method that was breathtakingly realistic and right, sought to break the universal dominion of Death over men.

Any person who has ever participated at a mass at which Father Berrigan is the celebrant is likely to be struck by his spontaneous yet deliberate manner. The spontaneity is conveyed in the *ex tempore* prayer, his refusal to use a liturgical book. But the deliberation is overwhelming, focusing as it does on his own, and every believer's, identification with Christ, not simply in baptism and by belief, but in living the pattern of dying and being raised again.

Apostolic Ministry: The Case of Martin Luther King Jr.

In Birmingham, Alabama, Fred Shuttlesworth, a Baptist pastor, led a boycott against white merchants in 1962, in order to protest continuing segregation. The Reverend Dr. Martin Luther King Jr. was addressing a group in support of this action when he was physically attacked by a young man who described himself as a Nazi. After his attacker was subdued, rather than insisting on an arrest, King asked that the man be allowed to sit down and listen to what was being said.

Although he was magnanimous with his attacker, King was an implacable opponent of the system of segregation. He wrote insistently to President Kennedy that January 1, 1963, the centenary of Lincoln's Emancipation Proclamation, would be the right time for a new declaration, "that segregation—a modern form of slavery—was morally and legally indefensible, that it was henceforth abolished, and that the federal government would use all its power to enforce the Negro's constitutional rights."[5] President Kennedy made no such declaration, and the situation in Birmingham worsened. Schools, buses, parks, and lunch counters were segregated, and opposition was met with arrest by officials and bombing by gangs. King announced in January of 1963 that he would lead demonstrations in Birmingham "until Pharaoh lets God's people go."

The resulting policy of sit-ins brought criticism, some from surprising quarters. Robert Kennedy called the campaign "ill-timed," and even local black leaders were unsympathetic. Finally, King himself was served with an injunction, prohibiting him from conducting demonstrations. He was arrested on Good Friday, April 12, 1963, and placed in solitary confinement. Although his arrest solidified black support, the Birmingham *News* printed a letter from eight white clergy, calling the demonstrations "unwise and untimely."

King wrote a famous response, his "Letter from Birmingham Jail," which opens with a comparison between King himself and the apostle Paul. The comparison was apt. King—like Paul—found himself in a minority, and King also aimed to advance beyond a principle Paul himself had cited.

In his letter to the Romans, Paul had called for obedience to those in authority, on the grounds that they were there to encourage the good and punish the wicked (see Romans 13:1–7). King replied:

> This is certainly a legitimate concern. Since we so diligently urge people to obey the Supreme Court's decision of 1954 outlawing segregation in the public schools, at first glance it may seem rather paradoxical for us consciously to break laws. One may well ask: "How can you advocate breaking some laws and obeying others?" The answer lies in the fact that there are two types of laws: just and unjust. I would be the first to advocate obeying just laws. One has not only a legal but a moral responsibility to obey just laws. Conversely, one has a moral responsibility to disobey unjust laws. I would agree with St. Augustine that "an unjust law is no law at all."

This principle of the overwhelming moral authority of God is as central to King's thought as his more famous dedication to nonviolence. He evolves his position in conscious interaction with the Christian tradition, but finally he claims to speak on personal authority; as he said prior to his arrest, it was "all that my life had brought me to be."

The events in Birmingham did not end with King's arrest, or with his release just over a week later. Although the right to demonstrate peacefully was finally upheld, and policies of desegregation were agreed upon among local leaders, that did not happen before official violence and mob violence mounted. At last, President Kennedy moved federal troops into position near the city, and announced his intention to bring civil rights legislation to Congress. The President of the United States invoked the example of the Emancipation Proclamation during a speech on June 11, and he went on to speak of what he called the moral issue at stake:

> One hundred years of delay have passed since President Lincoln freed the slaves, yet their heirs, their grandsons, are not fully free.

They are not yet freed from the bonds of injustice. They are not yet freed from social and economic oppression. And this nation, for all its hopes and all its boasts, will not be fully free until all its citizens are free.

Today that principle may seem to be obvious and even routine. In 1963, it was articulated at the price of suffering and death. And if it does seem a virtually self-evident truth today in the church, that is principally because we were provided with apostolic examples of what this truth looks like.

CONCLUSION

Speaking of the fourfold nature of the Gospels, Irenaeus compares them to the four quadrants of the heavens, the four principal winds that circle the world, the four cherubim before the throne of God. He even speaks of four covenants between God and humanity: Noah's, Abraham's, Moses', and Christ's (*Against Heresies* 3.9.8). His point is that the Gospels belong to the basics of life, and that the basics of life belong to the Gospels. His analysis stands as an account of the Christian tradition as a whole, if it is applied comprehensively: the richness of the operation of divine authority within the church may be understood along the lines of its appeal to Scripture, the rule of faith, the sacraments, and apostolic ministry.

Christianity is often difficult to understand, and difficulty often emerges between different denominations of Christians, because the grounds of authority are confused with literal texts. Christianity replaces literal textuality with texts that are used as instruments of God's Spirit. Written words, cherished traditions, empowering sacraments, and charismatic leaders may all convey that Spirit, but none can contain it.

JUDAISM

Judaism, the religion, identifies as its authoritative source "the Torah," or "the teaching," defined as God's revelation to Moses at Sinai. Writings deemed canonical enter the category of Torah, though into that same category also fall all authentic teachings of every age. The revelation myth of Judaism maintains that at Sinai God revealed the Torah in two media, written and oral. That is to say, while part of the revelation took written form, another part was formulated orally and transmitted through memorization. The tradition of Sinai may then come to concrete expression through any great sage's teaching. But the account of the position of Judaism set forth in these pages derives from the dual Torah, written and oral, as set forth in the Hebrew Scriptures and as interpreted by "our sages of blessed memory," the rabbis of the first seven centuries of the common era.

The Written Part of the Torah

We know the written part of the Torah as the Hebrew Scriptures of ancient Israel, or the "Old Testament." This is made up of the Pentateuch, or Five Books of Moses (Genesis, Exodus, Leviticus, Numbers, and Deuteronomy); the Former Prophets (Joshua, Judges, Samuel, and Kings); the Latter Prophets (Isaiah, Jeremiah, and Ezekiel); The Twelve Minor Prophets; and the Writings (Psalms, Proverbs, Job, Song of Songs (aka the Song of Solomon), Ruth, Lamentations, Ecclesiastes, Esther,

Daniel, Ezra, Nehemiah, and Chronicles). All translations from the written Torah come from the Revised Standard Version of the Bible.

The Oral Part of the Torah:
The Mishnah, Tosefta, and Two Talmuds

Judaism identifies a philosophical law code called the Mishnah (c. 200 C.E.) as the first and most important of the finally transcribed components of the oral Torah. The Mishnah is a set of rules in six parts, made up of laws dealing with the hierarchical classification of holy Israel in these categories: (1) agricultural life; (2) the holy calendar, Sabbaths, and festivals; (3) women and family; (4) civil law and the administration of justice and the state; (5) the Temple and its offerings; (6) purity laws. A tractate, or compilation of teachings, called Abot, "the Fathers," attached to the Mishnah, commences, "Moses received Torah at Sinai and handed it on to Joshua, Joshua to elders, and elders to prophets. And prophets handed it on to the men of the great assembly," and onward down to the very authorities of the Mishnah itself. That is how the document is placed within the oral tradition of Sinai. In addition to the Mishnah, three other writings carry forward the legal tradition of Sinai: the Tosefta (c. 300 C.E.), a set of further legal traditions in the model of those in the Mishnah; the Talmud of the Land of Israel (c. 400 C.E.), a systematic amplification of thirty-nine of the Mishnah's sixty-two topical tractates; and the Talmud of Babylonia (c. 600 C.E.), a commentary to thirty-seven of the same. The two Talmuds treat in common the second, third, and fourth divisions of the Mishnah. The former takes up the first; the latter, the fifth; and neither addresses the sixth. In addition, tractate Abot receives its Talmud in a compilation, the Fathers according to Rabbi Nathan, of indeterminate date.

The Oral Part of the Torah: Midrash-Compilations

The work of commenting on the Mishnah and its legal traditions found its counterpart, among the same sages or rabbis, in the labor of commenting on books of the written Torah. This work produced Midrash, or exegesis, meaning the interpretation of Scripture in light of contemporary events by appeal to a particular paradigm, or pattern, that showed how Scripture imposed meaning on contemporary occasions. Those biblical books selected for intensive amplification are the ones read in the synagogue: Genesis, in Genesis Rabbah (c. 400 C.E.); Exodus, in Mekhilta Attributed to Rabbi Ishmael (of indeterminate date but possibly c. 350 C.E.); Leviticus, in Sifra (c. 350 C.E.), and also in Leviticus Rabbah (c. 450 C.E.); Numbers, in Sifré to Numbers; and Deuteronomy, in Sifré to Deuteronomy (both c. 350 C.E.). In addition, Midrash-Compilations serve four of the scrolls read in synagogue worship: Lamentations, read on the 9th of Ab to commemorate the destruction of the Temple; Esther, read on Purim; Song of Songs, read on Passover; and Ruth, read on Pentecost. The Mishnah, Tosefta, Talmuds, and Midrash-Compilations together form the authoritative canon of Judaism in its formative age, the first seven centuries of the common era. All translations of portions of the oral Torah in this book come from those made by the author.

CHRISTIANITY

The Christian faith understands itself to be grounded in the Holy Spirit, God's self-communication. Access to the Holy Spirit is possible because in Jesus Christ God became human. The Incarnation (God becoming flesh, *caro* in Latin) is what provides the possibility of the Divine Spirit becoming accessible to the human spirit.

Speaking from the perspective of Christian faith, then, there is a single source of theology: the Holy Spirit, which comes from the Father and Son. But the inspiration of the Holy Spirit has been discovered and articulated by means of distinct kinds of literature in the history of the church. By becoming aware of the diversity of those sources, we can appreciate both the variety and the coherence of Christianity.

The Scriptures of Israel have always been valued within the church, both in Hebrew and in the Greek translation used in the Mediterranean world. (The Greek rendering is called the Septuagint, after the seventy translators who were said to have produced it.) Those were the only scriptures of the church in its primitive phase, when the New Testament was being composed. In their meetings of prayer and worship, followers of Jesus saw the Scriptures of Israel "fulfilled" by their faith: their conviction was that the same Spirit of God that was active in the prophets was, through Christ, available to them.

The New Testament was produced in primitive communities of Christians to prepare people for baptism, to order worship, to resolve disputes, to encourage faith, and for like purposes. As a whole, it is a collective document of primitive Christianity. Its purpose is to call out and order true Israel in response to the triumphant news of Jesus' preaching, activity, death, and Resurrection. The New Testament provides the means of accessing the Spirit spoken of in the Scriptures of Israel. Once the New Testament was formed, it was natural to refer to the Scriptures of Israel as the "Old Testament."

The Old Testament is classic for Christians because it represents the ways in which God's Spirit might be known. At the same time, the New Testament is normative: it sets out how we actually appropriate the Spirit of God, which is also the spirit of Christ. That is why the Bible as a whole is accorded a place of absolute privilege in the Christian tradition: it is the literary source from which we know both how the Spirit of God has been known and how we can appropriate it.

The term "Early Christianity" designates the time between the second and the fourth centuries of the common era, the period during which the church founded its theology on the basis of the scriptures of the Old and New Testaments. Although Christians were under extreme—sometimes violent—pressure from the Roman Empire, Early Christianity was a time of unique creativity. From thinkers as different from one another as Bishop Irenaeus in France and Origen, the speculative teacher active first in Egypt and then in Palestine, a common Christian philosophy began to emerge. The period of Early Christianity might also be called a "catholic" phase, in the sense that it was characterized by a quest for a "general" or "universal" account of the faith, but that designation may lead to confusion with Roman Catholicism at a later stage, and is avoided here.

After the Roman Empire itself embraced Christianity in the fourth century, the church was in a position to articulate formally its understanding of the faith by means of common standards. During this period of Orthodox Christianity, correct norms of worship, baptism, creeds, biblical texts, and doctrines were established. From Augustine in the West to Gregory of Nyssa in the East, Christianity for the first and only time in its history approached being truly ecumenical.

The collapse of Rome under the barbarian invasions in the West broke the unity of the church. Although the East remained wedded to the forms of Orthodoxy (and accepts them to this day), the West developed its own structure of governance and its own theology, especially after Charlemagne was crowned as emperor of the Romans by Pope Leo III on Christmas day in 800 C.E.

To severe arguments regarding political jurisdiction, East and West added doctrinal divisions. The pope was condemned in 876 by a synod in Constantinople for failing to stop a small change in the wording of the Nicene Creed, which had become accepted in the West. A papal legate in 1054 excommunicated the patriarch of Constantinople. Even that act pales in comparison with what happened in 1204: European Crusaders on their way to Jerusalem sacked and pillaged Constantinople itself.

European Christianity flourished during the Middle Ages, and Scholastic theology was a result of that success. The Scholastics were organized on the basis of educational centers, Thomas Aquinas at the University of Paris during the thirteenth century being the best example. During the periods of Early Christianity and Orthodoxy, theologies as well as forms of discipline and worship were developed for the first time. Scholastic theology was in the position of systematizing these developments for the usage of the West. At the same time, Scholastic theologians also rose to the challenge of explaining Christian faith in the terms of the new philosophical movements they came into contact with.

The Reformation, between the sixteenth and the eighteenth centuries, challenged the very idea of a single system of Christianity. Martin Luther imagined that each region might settle on its own form of religion. In England the settlement was on a national basis, while in John Calvin's Geneva the elders of the city made that determination. But in all its variety, the Reformation insisted that the Bible and worship should be put into the language of the people, and that their governance should be consistent with their faith.

From the eighteenth century until the present, Christianity in its modern form has been wrestling with the consequences of the rise of rationalism and science. The results have been diverse and surprising. They include Protestant Fundamentalism—a claim that the Bible articulates certain "fundamentals," which govern human existence—and the Roman Catholic idea of papal infallibility, the claim that the pope may speak the truth of the church without error. In both cases, the attempt is made to establish an axiom of reason that reason itself may not challenge. But modern Christianity also includes a vigorous acceptance of the primacy of individual judgment in the life of communities: examples include the Confessing Church in Germany, which opposed the Third Reich, and the current movement of Liberation Theology in Central and South America.

Today Christians may use many combinations of the sort of sources named here to articulate their beliefs, and the resulting pattern is likely to be as distinctive as what has been produced in the past.

ISLAM

The Qur'ān

The single source that constitutes the basis of all inquiry into the religion of Islam is the Qur'ān. Revealed to the Prophet Muḥammad from 610 to 632 C.E., it is understood as God's own speech. That is to say, Muslims believe that the Qur'ān is not merely inspired by God, it is exactly what God meant to say to the early Muslim community and to the world in general. Furthermore, God spoke to Muḥammad (usually through the angel Gabriel) in Arabic, and to this day Muslims resist translation of the Qur'ān into any other language. The Qur'ān is about as long as the Christian New Testament. It is divided into 114 chapters (called *suras*), which range in size from a few verses to a few hundred. All but one of these suras begins with an invocation, "In the name of God, the Merciful, the Compassionate," and with these words pious Muslims begin all endeavors of importance. There are many translations of the Qur'ān into English; that of A. J. Arberry[1] is widely recognized as the best and will be used in this series, despite the unfortunate gender bias in Arberry's language.

The Qur'ān describes itself as a continuation and perfection of a tradition of revelation that began with the Torah, revealed to the Jews, and the Gospels, revealed to the Christians. In fact, the Qur'ān directly addresses Jews and Christians, urging them to put aside their differences and join Muslims in the worship of the one, true God: "Say: People of the Book! Come now to a word common between us and you, that we serve none but God" (The House of Imran. 3:56). Jesus and Moses are explicitly recognized as prophets, and the rules and pious regulations in the Qur'ān fit in well with similar rules found in Judaism and Christianity. Of course, a special role is given to Muḥammad, the seal of the prophets and the leader of the early Muslim community.

Sunna: The Prophet as Text

The Prophet Muḥammad serves as the second "text" for Muslims. Unlike the Qur'ān, which is the single source for God's divine word in Islam, the words and deeds of the Prophet are found in many different sources. When it comes to the Prophet, precise words are not as important as his general "way of doing things"; in Arabic, this is called the Prophet's *sunna.*

The Prophet Muḥammad ibn 'Abd Allāh was born almost six centuries after Jesus' birth, around 570 c.e., and for the first forty years of his life he organized trading caravans. Around the year 610, he began meditating in a cave near his hometown of Mecca. During these meditations he was overwhelmed by a vision of the angel Gabriel commanding him, "Recite!" This event changed his life forever and he began, slowly, to preach to his relatives and neighbors. After years of effort, Muḥammad and a small group of followers moved to the town of Medina. This *Hijra,* the emigration of Muslims from Mecca to Medina in 622 c.e., marks the beginning of the Muslim calendar and was a turning point for the early community. In Medina, hundreds flocked to the new religion, and when the Prophet died in 632, he left behind thousands of believers. The survival of this early group is testified to by the almost one billion Muslims in the world today. Now, as then, Muslims see the Prophet as an example of the ideal believer. Muslims often name their boys after the Prophet, wear clothes like his, and try to live according to his precepts.

Hadith: Examples of the Prophet's Sunna

Muḥammad's words and deeds were preserved and passed on from generation to generation in a form of oral transmission known as hadith. The Arabic word *ḥadīth* means "story," and a typical hadith begins with a list of those from whom the story was received, going back in time to the Prophet. Following this list is the story itself, often an account of the Prophet's actions in a particular situation or the Prophet's advice on a certain problem. The list of transmitters is an integral part of the hadith; for example: "al-Qāsim—ʿĀʾisha—The Prophet said . . ." Here, al-Qāsim (an early legal scholar) transmitted this hadith from ʿĀʾisha (one of the Prophet's wives), who heard it directly from the Prophet. These stories were quite popular among early generations of Muslims, but no one attempted to collect and organize them until over a hundred years after the Prophet's death. Two important early collections of hadith are those by al-Bukhārī (d. 870) and Muslim ibn al-Ḥajjāj (d. 875). Hadith are also found in works of history and in commentaries on the Qurʾān. It is worth emphasizing that Muslims do not believe that Muḥammad was divine. A careful distinction was maintained between divine words, which originated with God and therefore were put into the Qurʾān, and Muḥammad's general advice to his community. Both sets of words were spoken by the Prophet, but the first were written down and carefully preserved, while the second were handed down through the more informal vehicle of hadith.

Tafsīr: Commentary on the Texts

Today, as in previous ages, Muslims often turn directly to the Qurʾān and hadith for guidance and inspiration, but just as often, they turn to commentaries and interpretations of these primary sources. These commentaries concern themselves with questions of grammar, context, and the legal and mystical implications of the text. They expand the original source, often collecting interpretations of many previous generations together. The results can be massive. The Qur'ān, for instance, is only one volume, but a typical commentary can be twenty volumes or more. The importance of commentary in the Islamic tradition demonstrates that the Qur'ān and sunna of the Prophet are not the only sources for guidance in Islam. Rather, Muslims have depended on learned men and women to interpret the divine sources and add their own teachings to this tradition. Therefore, these commentaries are valuable sources for understanding the religious beliefs of Muslims throughout the ages. Together with the Qur'ān and hadith, they provide a continuous expression of Islamic religious writing from scholars, mystics, and theologians from over fourteen centuries.

BUDDHISM

Upon examining the major bodies of sacred literature in Buddhism, it must first be noted that Buddhism does not define "canon" in the same sense that the Judaic, Christian, and Islamic religions do. First of all, scriptures comprising a Buddhist canon are not deemed authoritative on the basis of being regarded as an exclusive revelation granted to humans by a supreme divine being. In principle, the ultimate significance of a given scriptural text for Buddhists lies less in the source from whom it comes, or in the literal meanings of its words, than in its ability to generate an awakening to the true nature of reality. Texts are principally valued according to their ability to enable one to engage in practices leading to an enlightened state of salvific insight, which liberates one from suffering, although they can also be utilized to serve other vitally important if less ultimate purposes, such as the cultivation of compassionate ethics, explication of philosophical issues, and protection from obstacles to personal well-being. Buddhism is also distinctive in that it has never established any one body that has functioned in an equivalent manner to the Rabbinate, Episcopate, or Caliphate, charged with the determination of a single, fixed, closed list of authoritative works for the entire tradition. On a local level, Buddhist canons, based on the hermeneutical standard of privileging the realization of enlightenment over source and word, have tended to remain open (to varying degrees) to the inclusion of new scriptures over the course of history.

It should not be concluded that the factors discussed above have ever substantially limited the amount of sacred literature produced in Buddhism, or have relegated scripture to a status less than primary in the religion's history. On the contrary, the various major Buddhist collections of scripture are extraordinarily voluminous in size[2] and have continuously occupied a most highly revered place in the tradition as primary sources of teaching. Appeals to a scripture's provenance have indeed played a momentous role in Buddhist history, with a primary determinate of a text's canonicity being recognition of it as containing *buddha-vacana,* the "spoken word" of a Buddha, or enlightened being—usually Siddhartha Gautama, or Shākyamuni Buddha (563–483 B.C.E.)—the Indian founder of the religion. To reiterate, one can be sure that the authority assigned to buddha-vacana is derived in part from its source, but what is of utmost import is its liberating power as an indicator of enlightened wisdom.

Insofar as we can determine it, the buddha-vacana, first transmitted shortly after the end of Shakyamuni Buddha's life by his main disciples, at first came to consist of two major sets of texts. The first set is known as Sutra (Sūtra), and it is comprised of the discourses of the Buddha (or in some cases of his disciples, but with his sanction), relating the events in his past and present lifetimes and his practical and philosophical teachings. The second set, known as the Vinaya, presents the ethical discipline and monastic rules that regulate the life of the *sangha,* or community, as they were laid down by the Buddha. Collectively, these two sets form the core of what is known as Dharma, or Buddhist doctrine.

In addition, Buddhist canons include texts that provide further explanation and guidance in the Dharma, such as commentaries on the Sutra and Vinaya, treatises on philosophical topics, and ritual and meditative manuals. Broadly known as Shastra (Śāstra), or exegesis, this type of work derived its authority not from being buddha-vacana, but from being authored by those scholiasts, philosophers, and meditation masters who came to be regarded by later Buddhists as of the highest accomplishments and explicatory skills. Perhaps the most important genre of Shastra texts is the collections known as Abhidharma ("Further Dharma"), which consist of systematic analyses and classifications of doctrine composed by scholastic masters as early as 300 years after the Buddha.

Despite general agreement among Buddhist traditions on the principle that the words of a Buddha and the further exegeses by great masters of philosophy and meditation are what constitute authority and canonicity, there has also been profound disagreement among these traditions about conceptions of what a Buddha is and what a Buddha teaches, and in turn about which masters best explicated the most efficacious and reliable means to liberation. In addition to such sectarian differences, various regional and linguistic divisions have contributed to the compilation of a number of separate canons. Thus, in speaking of the major sources of Buddhism that will inform these volumes, it is necessary to briefly identify the religion's major sectarian and regional divisions.

The Buddhist world today can be divided according to three major traditions, each of which traces its origins to developments in India, presently inhabits a more or less definable geographic region outside India, and subscribes to a distinctive body of scriptural sources, which the followers regard as the most authentic version of the Dharma. The Theravada (Theravāda) ("Teaching of the Elders") tradition was the first of the three to historically form a distinct community (fourth century C.E.), and today it continues to thrive in the countries of Sri Lanka, Thailand, Myanmar (Burma), Laos, and Cambodia. The Theravada corpus of scripture—known as the Tripiṭaka ("Three Baskets") because of its division into the three sections of Sutra, Vinaya, and Abhidharma, described above—was rendered into written form in the Pali language by Sri Lankan elders in the first century B.C.E., but its origins are traced back to a council convened shortly after the end of the Buddha's life in the early fifth century B.C.E., during which his leading disciples orally recited the Buddha's words and began committing them to memory. Theravadins regard their texts as conserving the Dharma as it was originally taught and practiced by Shakyamuni and his most accomplished followers, who are known as *arhat*s, or "worthy ones." Their Tripitaka establishes fundamental Buddhist teachings on the nature of suffering, the selflessness of persons, the impermanence of all phenomena, and the path of nonviolent ethics and meditation, which leads to liberating wisdom.

The second major Buddhist tradition—which has called itself the Mahayana (Mahāyāna) ("Great Vehicle") because it has seen its teachings as superior to those of the Theravada and the other (now defunct) preceding early Indian schools—developed in the first centuries of the common era in North India and Central Asia, and has long since come to be the predominant form of Buddhism followed in the East Asian countries of China, Korea, Vietnam, and Japan. While the content of the Vinaya and Abhidharma portions of its canon is closely modeled (with notable exceptions) on texts from the earlier Indian schools (which Mahayanists have labeled collectively as Hinayana (Hīnayāna) or "Small Vehicle"), the Mahayana also presented a new, divergent scriptural dispensation in its Sutra literature. Composed originally in Sanskrit, these Mahayana sutras were said to be a higher form of buddha-vacana, which had been kept from the inferior Hinayana Buddhists until the capabilities of humans had evolved enough to employ this more difficult, but also more efficacious, Dharma. Popular texts such as the *Perfection of Wisdom, Lotus, Teaching of Vimalakirti, Flower Garland, Descent into Lanka,* and *Pure Land* Sutras promoted a new spiritual ideal, the career of the paragon figure of compassion and insight, the *bodhisattva* ("enlightenment being"). Focusing on the philosophical and practical tenets espoused in these newly emergent sutras, the great Indian masters of the first millennium of the common era composed explicatory treatises that would come to stand as centerpieces in the Mahayana canons. Most important are the works of the Madhyamika (Mādhayamika), or "Middle Way," school, which expounded on the central idea of *shunyata,* or "emptiness," and those of the Yogacara (Yogācāra) ("Yoga Practice") school, which developed influential theories on the mind and its construction of objective realities. The subsequent history of Mahayana as it was transformed in East Asia is a complex and varied one, but in the long run two practically oriented schools, namely the Pure Land and Meditation (commonly known in the West by its Japanese name, Zen) schools, emerged as the most popular and remain so today. These schools supplement their canons with texts containing the discourses and dialogues of their respective patriarchs.

The third Buddhist tradition to appear on the historical scene, beginning around the sixth century C.E., is the Vajrayana (Vajrayāna) ("Thunderbolt Vehicle"), commonly known as Tantric Buddhism. The Vajrayana survives today in the greater Tibetan cultural areas of Asia, including the Himalayan kingdoms of Sikkim, Nepal, and Bhutan. Tantric Buddhists regard themselves as Mahayanists, and include in their canon all of the major Mahayana texts mentioned above. However, the Vajrayana itself also claimed a new and divergent dispensation of the Buddha's word, in the form of texts called Tantras. While not philosophically innovative, the Tantras offered novel systems of meditative disciplines and ritual practices known as *sādhanas.* Followers of the Vajrayana maintain that the Tantras are the highest and final words of the Buddha, esoterically preserved until the circumstances were right for their exposure to humanity. As the name *Vajrayana* suggests, the uniqueness of the Tantras lies in their claim to be providing the most powerful and expeditious means of attaining enlightenment. Like their East Asian Mahayana counterparts, Tantric Buddhists also reserve a place of eminence in their canons for the compositions of their most accomplished masters, who are known as *mahāsiddhas,* or "great adepts."

HINDUISM

What we in the twentieth century call Hinduism is in fact a set of religious practices that have developed over three thousand years of Indian history and have a great variety of textual sources. That history begins with the four Vedas—oral compositions of people who called themselves Aryans and who were the ancestors of many of the inhabitants of India today. The term *Veda* means "knowledge," and these four works comprise the accompaniment to Vedic sacrifice—the main form of worship for the early Aryans. Sacrifice usually involved an animal or vegetable offering to one of the many Vedic gods. The first Veda, the *Rig Veda (Ṛg Veda),* is the oldest (c. 1500 B.C.E.), and comprises the mythological hymns of the sacrifice. The second, the *Yajur Veda, (Yajur Veda)* contains directions on how to conduct the ritual; the third, the *Sama Veda (Sāma Veda),* contains accompanying musical chants. The final Veda, the *Atharva Veda,* includes hymns for fertility, healing, and other everyday uses in the domestic context, apart from the public sacrifice.

The second set of works important to Hinduism is more

philosophical in nature. These works are the Upanishads (Upaniṣads) (c. 900–300 B.C.E.), and consist of speculation about the power behind the sacrifice, called *brahman*, and the nature of the sacrificing self, called *atman* (*ātman*). The Upanishads also contain the beginnings of a system of belief in reincarnation—more properly called the transmigration of the individual self—through the endless cycle of births, deaths, and sufferings, called *samsara* (*saṁsāra*). The Upanishadic philosophers believed that the key to liberation from this cycle of suffering was the union between the atman and brahman. Around 200 B.C.E., these initial ideas were developed into an elaborate science of meditation called Yoga, by the philosopher Patañjali. His treatise, the *Yoga Sutras* (*Yoga Sūtras*), inaugurated the system of *yoga* as we know and practice it today.

While the Vedas, Upanishads, and *Yoga Sutras* reflect the religious practices of the upper strata, or castes, of Indian society there was very little textual evidence for popular religious practices until the emergence of the epics, the *Mahabharata* (*Mahābhārata*) and the *Ramayana* (*Rāmāyāṇa*). The *Mahabharata* is the story of the tragic war between cousins, the Kauravas and the Pandavas (Paṇḍavas). The *Ramayana* depicts the exploits of Rama (Rāma)—a hero said to be the *avatar* (*avatāra*), or manifestation, of the god Vishnu (Viṣṇu). In rescuing his wife Sita (Sītā) from the demon Ravana (Rāvaṇa), Rama slays Ravana and rids the world of the evil. Many see these two epics as the source of popular theology prevalent in India today. They are the first texts that make extensive mention of the classical Hindu pantheon—Shiva (Śiva), Vishnu (Viṣṇu), Brahma (Brahmā), and Devi (Devī), or the goddess. The *Mahabharata* is also the source of the *Bhagavad Gita* (*Bhagavad Gītā*)—the *Song to the Lord Krishna,* who, in human form, acts as a charioteer in the war. Particularly in the nineteenth and twentieth centuries, the *Bhagavad Gita* has inspired much popular devotion as a Hindu response to the Christian missionary movement.

Near the end of the period of the composition of the epics (c. 200 C.E.), many kings, especially in North India, began to patronize these popular deities and build temples to house them. Such temples had texts called Puranas (Purāṇas) attached to them; the term *purāṇa* literally means "story of the olden times." Puranas are encyclopedic compilations that praised the exploits of particular deities—Vishnu, Shiva, Brahma, and the Devi, mentioned above. Notoriously difficult to date, the Puranas range from 200 C.E. to 1700 C.E. Another important set of texts, called Dharma Shastras (Dharma Śāstras), emerged at about this period; these were elaborate law books that codified daily life according to rules concerned with purity and pollution. The most famous of these is the *Manavadharmashastra* (*Mānava-dharma-Śāstra*), or the *Laws of Manu*. The Puranas and the Dharma Shastras provide the bulk of the material upon which the modern Hindu tradition draws, and they originate in all regions of India.

The wide geographical spread of the Puranas is partly due to the fact that devotional movements were not exclusive to the northern Gangetic plain, where the Vedas and Upanishads were composed, but were inspired equally by the South Indian, or Dravidian, civilizations. These devotional movements were called *bhakti,* literally meaning "belonging to." A *bhakta* is someone who "belongs to" a particular god, and has chosen that god for devotion. Beginning in the eighth century C.E., the South Indian bhaktas wrote poetry that became an influential source for Hinduism. The collection of poems by the Tamil saint Nammalvar (Nammāḷvār), the Tiruvaymoli (*Tiruvāy-moḷi*), has attained the same canonical status as the Vedas, and is called the Tamil Veda. In addition, the Bengali saint Caitanya inspired a bhakti movement devoted to Krishna (Kṛṣṇa) in the late fifteenth century C.E.; his followers wrote treatises, among them the *Haribhaktirasamrtasindhu,* and *Haribhaktivilasa,* that explain the theology and ritual of devotion to Krishna. Many northern and western Indian poets, such as Mirabai (Mīrā Bai) (b. c. 1420 C.E.) and Tukaram (Tukārām) (1608–1649 C.E.), have contributed significantly to the huge corpus of bhakti poetry and theology that Hindus read and recite today.

The final major source for the study of Hinduism is the Vedanta (Vedānta) philosophical tradition, whose development and systematization is attributed to the teacher Shankara (Śaṅkara) in the ninth century C.E. Shankara, and his major successor, Ramanuja (Rāmānuja) (twelfth century C.E.), developed their philosophy through commentaries, called *bhasyas,* on the two main texts of Vedanta—the *Vedanta Sutras* (*Vedanta Sūtras*) and the *Brahma Sutras* (*Brahma Sūtras*). These texts summarize the doctrine of the Upanishads, mentioned above. In his classic work, *Brahmasutrabhashya* (*Brahmasūtrabhāsya*), Shankara argues a philosophy of nonduality (*advaita*). For him, the perceptions of the mind and the senses are simply *avidya* (*avidyā*), ignorance. In ignorance, we perceive a duality between subject and object, self and the source of self. This perception of duality prevents the self (atman) from complete identity with brahman. When complete identity is achieved, however, there is liberation of the self from all ignorance.

These manifold sources—the Vedas, the Upanishads, the epics, the Puranas, the Dharma Shastras, the diverse corpus of bhakti poetry, and Vedanta philosophy—make up the spiritual foundations of Hindu practice today.

2. ISLAM

1. Muḥammad b. Idrīs al-Shāfiʿī, *al-Risāla fī uṣūl al-fiqh*, trans. Majid Khadduri as *Islamic Jurisprudence: Shāfiʿī's Risāla* (reprint, Cambridge: Islamic Texts Society, 1987), 67–68. Subsequent textual references, unless otherwise noted, are to this source.

2. Mālik b. Anas, *al-Muwaṭṭaʾ*, ed. Ḥasan ʿAbdallāh Sharaf (Cairo: Dār al-Rayān, 1988), 2:147–48. Subsequent textual references are to this source.

3. Muḥammad b. Idrīs al-Shāfiʿī, *al-Risālah,* ed. Aḥmad Shākir (Cairo: Maktabat Dār al-Turāth, 1979), 73–75.

4. Abū Ḥāmid al-Ghazzālī, *Iḥyāʾ ʿulūm al-dīn* (Beirut: Dār al-Fikr, 1991), 1:27–28. Subsequent textual references are to this source.

5. al-Ṭabarī, *The History of al-Ṭabarī,* vol. 6, trans. W. Montgomery Watt as *Muhammad at Mecca* (Albany: State University of New York Press, 1988), 71. Subsequent textual references are to this source.

6. Ibn Isḥāq, *The Life of Muhammad,* trans. A. Guillaume (Karachi: Oxford University Press, 1978), 555. Subsequent textual references are to this source.

7. A. J. Arberry, *The Koran Interpreted* (New York: Macmillan, 1955), 2:8.

8. Elizabeth Fernea, *Guests of the Sheik* (New York: Doubleday, 1965), 115.

3. BUDDHISM

1. Reginald Ray, "Buddhism: Sacred Text Written and Realized," in *The Holy Book in Comparative Perspective,* ed. Frederick M. Denny and Rodney L. Taylor (Columbia: University of South Carolina Press, 1985).

2. The word *piṭaka* or "basket," as in the term *Tri-piṭaka* ("Three Baskets"), connotes a collection of texts.

4. HINDUISM

1. This and other quotations from the Manusmṛti are taken from *The Laws of Manu,* trans. Wendy Doniger with Brian K. Smith (London: Penguin Books, 1991).

2. From *The Rig Veda: An Anthology,* trans. Wendy Doniger O'Flaherty (Harmondsworth, Middlesex, England: Penguin Books Ltd., 1981), 30.

3. *Tantravārttika of Kumārila Bhaṭṭa,* ed. and trans. G. Jha (Calcutta: Bibliotheca Indica, 1924), 165.

4. From John Carman and Vasudha Narayanan, *The Tamil Veda: Piḷḷān's Interpretation of the Tiruvāymoḷi* (Chicago: University of Chicago Press, 1989), 6.

5. Rammohun Roy, cited in D. Killingley, "Rammohun Roy's Interpretation of the Vedanta" (Ph.D. thesis, London School of Oriental and African Studies, 1977), 341.

6. *The Bhagavad Gītā: Krishna's Counsel in Time of War,* trans. Barbara Stoler Miller (New York: Bantam Books, 1986), 50.

7. *Sources of Indian Tradition,* 2d ed., vol. 1, ed. and rev. Ainslie T. Embree (New York: Columbia University Press, 1988), 350–51.

8. Ibid., 362–63.

5. CHRISTIANITY

1. Dietrich Bonhoeffer, *Ethics,* trans. E. Bethge (New York: Macmillan, 1965), 354.

2. Ibid., 357.

3. See *The Documents of Vatican II,* ed. W. M. Abbott (New York: Guild, 1966), 137.

4. See William Stringfellow and Anthony Towne, *Suspect Tenderness: The Ethics of the Berrigan Witness* (New York: Holt, Rinehart and Winston, 1971), 8, 6–7.

5. For this and other quotations see Stephen B. Oates, *Let the Trumpet Sound: The Life of Martin Luther King, Jr.* (New York: Harper and Row, 1982), 205–76.

LITERARY SOURCES OF THE WORLD RELIGIONS

1. A. J. Arberry, *The Koran Interpreted* (New York: Macmillan, 1955).
2. For example, a version of the Chinese Buddhist canon, published in Tokyo in the 1920s, is made up of fifty-five Western-style volumes totaling 2,148 texts!